Family Recipes
from Rosedown & Catalpa
Plantations

Family Recipes from Rosedown & Catalpa Plantations

BY
RICHARD SCOTT
STELLA PITTS
MARY THOMPSON

PELICAN PUBLISHING COMPANY
Gretna 2005

Library of Congress Cataloging-in-Publication Data

Scott, Richard, 1944-
  Family recipes from Rosedown and Catalpa plantations / by Richard Scott,
Stella Pitts, Mary Thompson.
      p. cm.
  ISBN 978-1-58980-211-7 (alk. paper)
  1.   Cookery, American--Louisiana style.   I. Pitts, Stella, 1937- II.
Thompson, Mary, 1946- III. Title.

  TX715.2.L68S36 2005
  641.59763--dc22

                                    2004023768

Printed in the United States of America
Published by Pelican Publishing Company, Inc.
1000 Burmaster Street, Gretna, Louisiana 70053

Table of Contents

———◦•◦———

Acknowledgments

——•••——

The authors of this cookbook express gratitude to the following individuals for their generous assistance in the creation of this cookbook: Paul C. Kiene, historical cooking consultant, former proprietor of the Orange Grove Plantation Store, and generous donor to the Rosedown Kitchen; Thomas W. Klein, antiquarian, St. Francisville, Louisiana; Charlen Simmons Moore, researcher and former interpretive ranger, Rosedown Plantation State Historic Site; W. Parke Moore III, site manager, Rosedown Plantation State Historic Site; Jill Larsen, artist and photographer, New Orleans, Louisiana; Polly Luttrull, curator, Rosedown Plantation State Historic Site.

Introduction

———◆———

After nearly half a century of emptiness and silence, the old plantation kitchen at Rosedown has come to life again.

Today, the fire blazes again in the ancient fireplace; iron kettles hang from the old crane, filled with boiling vegetables and meats; close to the fire, two chickens roast slowly in the old "tin kitchen" utensil; and down on the brick hearth, on top of a bed of hot coals, Martha Turnbull's white cake rises slowly in an iron kettle beneath a cover piled with more hot coals.

The once-a-week cooking demonstrations at Rosedown provide

Rosedown Plantation House.

visitors to the state-owned historic site with a tantalizing glimpse of the nineteenth century cooking procedures followed for many years on this historic Louisiana plantation. Visitors also can see for themselves—and sometimes even taste—the quaint, old-fashioned, and sometimes all-but-forgotten dishes enjoyed by Martha and Daniel Turnbull and their family and friends so long ago.

Historians and preservationists have long known that the past can never be recreated exactly as it really was, but the cooking demonstrations at Rosedown come very close, providing a fascinating—and delicious—glimpse of an era that is gone.

This cookbook is an outgrowth of these cooking demonstrations and also is a means of recording and preserving a selection of several hundred Turnbull family recipes, or receipts as they were called, recently discovered in the attic of nearby Catalpa Plantation, a site closely connected with the family and history of Rosedown. These

Catalpa Plantation House.

receipts, along with many other hand-written Turnbull family receipts, are used in the Rosedown kitchen demonstrations and are typical of plantation cookery practiced throughout the antebellum and post-bellum South.

The names of these early Southern concoctions are intriguing and delightful: jumbles and puffs, tomatoe soy and monkey pudding, lightning cake and foolish pie.

And where did the Turnbull family find these receipts? Many probably came from their relatives—Martha's family was originally from England, Daniel's came from Scotland. Like all early Southern families, they also exchanged receipts with friends and nearby neighbors in West Feliciana Parish. They often copied receipts they especially liked in nineteenth century cookbooks, such as *Miss Leslie's Seventy-Five Receipts for Pastry, Cakes and Sweetmeats,* published in 1827, and *Miss Leslie's Directions for Cookery,* published in 1851. Martha Turnbull owned both of these early American cookbooks penned by the famous Eliza Leslie of Philadelphia.

Some Turnbull family receipts may even have originated at Mount

Rosedown Kitchen.

Vernon, home of America's first president, George Washington. The Turnbull's oldest son, William, married Caroline Butler, whose grandmother was Eleanor Parke Custis Lewis, the famous "Nellie," and whose great-grandmother was Martha Washington herself. Both Nellie and Martha were famous cooks, and many of their original receipts have been preserved, including one of the most famous American receipts, Martha's receipt for "Great Cake," which begins with the words, "Take forty eggs and divide the whites from the yolks . . . "

Hand-written receipts were common in many Southern homes, shared among family and friends and eventually passed down to subsequent generations. Sadly, far too many of these irreplaceable bits of Southern culinary history were lost through the years—forgotten in attic trunks, damaged in fires and storms, left behind when families moved away, or simply discarded by later generations. It is therefore truly remarkable that so many of the Turnbull family's receipts have survived to provide a valuable record of this Louisiana plantation family's dining habits.

Food prepared in the Rosedown kitchen.

Established shortly after the state of Louisiana acquired Rosedown Plantation in late 2000, the cooking program was begun by former interpretive park ranger Richard Scott and has been continued by staff members and volunteers, who keep the fires going, cook the dishes, and give visitors an oral history of plantation cooking—its origins, its traditions, and the lasting influence it has had on modern cooking methods and cuisine, not only in the South but throughout the entire country.

The Rosedown Plantation kitchen, like all plantation kitchens, was always separate from the main house, primarily because of the danger of fire but also to keep the heat and smells of cooking far from the house. The meals were cooked here, then carried on covered platters into the service room at the rear of mansion, where they were arranged on serving pieces and carried into the dining room.

Many of the old iron and tin utensils used at Rosedown are original nineteenth century cooking items—kettles and skillets, gridirons and toasters, trivets and graters and corn shellers, long-handled spoons and forks. There are wooden "beadles" (today known as potato mashers) and a "tin kitchen" that is a forerunner of a modern rotisserie oven. Simple and primitive as they all are, they really work, to the amazement and delight of visitors.

Of course, missing from this living portrait of a vital part of nineteenth century plantation life are the people who actually worked in the kitchen and produced the daily meals for the family so long ago— the slave cooks. Ranked at the very top of the plantation's slave hierarchy, the slave cooks were highly valued and skillful members of the plantation community. Working under the direction of their mistresses, they provided astonishingly diverse and delicious meals under difficult and often uncomfortable circumstances that modern-day cooks can scarcely imagine.

In 1862, an inventory of slaves at Rosedown Plantation listed two cooks—a forty-year-old man named Wilkinson and a woman named Grace, who was fifty. Nothing more is known of them, nor do we know all the names or the histories of their predecessors or of those who followed after them.

But names can make people from the past seem very real, and it is somehow easy to imagine Wilkinson and Grace as they might have been at Rosedown in 1862: building up the fire, piling up the hot coals, peeling vegetables and mixing puddings, and stirring cake and bread batters. They worked from early morning until late in the evening, day after day, summer and winter. They prepared early morning breakfasts, main meals that were served at three o'clock in the afternoon, and light evening suppers that closed out the long plantation day.

In the hope that Grace and Wilkinson, and all of their fellow slave cooks throughout the plantation South, will always be remembered for their skills and their lasting contributions to Southern cooking, we dedicate this volume to them: to Grace and Wilkinson of Rosedown Plantation and to all the slave cooks who lived and labored in the plantation kitchens of the antebellum South.

Richard Scott, Stella Pitts, and Mary Thompson

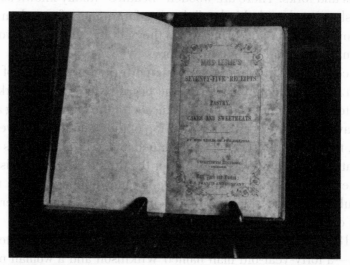

Martha Turnbull's copy of Miss Leslie's Seventy-Five Receipts *cookbook.*

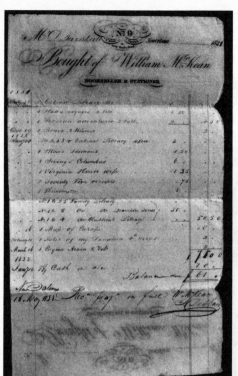

New Orleans bill of sale for Daniel Turnbull's purchase of books and library equipment in 1831-32. It included copies of The Virginia Housewife and Seventy-Five Receipts *cookbooks for Martha Turnbull.*

An original Rosedown nineteenth-century gridiron and grater in the kitchen.

A cook in the kitchen at an unknown Louisiana plantation. Image taken from a glass plate negative, second half of the nineteenth century.

Rosedown and Catalpa:
The Story of Two Plantations

Rosedown and Catalpa—two legendary names in West Feliciana Parish, two very different plantation houses that share a common heritage as well as a fascinating history that reaches back to the earliest days of the nineteenth century.

Both houses have close connections with two of the most prominent early plantation families in the region—the Barrows and the Forts. Both were originally surrounded by plantations comprising thousands of acres of cotton and sugar cane. Both were renowned in the region for the wealth, culture, and hospitality of the families who owned them. And both, in different ways, are survivors—reminders of a vanished way of life that have emerged beautiful and vibrant in the twenty-first century.

It was at the very beginning of the nineteenth century—in 1800—that two North Carolina families, the Barrows and the Forts, arrived in "Neuva Feliciana," a stronghold of the English in a predominantly French and Spanish territory. The Barrows became one of the wealthiest and most prominent families of the Old South, as influential in Louisiana as were the Byrds, the Carters, and the Lees in Virginia. The Forts, cousins to the Barrows, became some of the most prominent planters in Louisiana, owning numerous plantations and hundreds of slaves.

Leading the Barrow family to Louisiana was the widowed Olivia Ruffin Barrow, with her two sons, Robert and William, and her daughter, Mary.

Olivia Barrow is buried in the family cemetery at Highland, the earliest Barrow house still standing in the region and still occupied by descendents of the original builder, Olivia's son, William Barrow III. The house was known in the beginning as Locust Grove and is believed to be the first example of Federal-style architecture built in the Feliciana region.

The gardens at Highland were once extensive and spectacular, and the plantation included an enormous sugarhouse, a racetrack, a dance hall for the slaves, a slave hospital, and numerous other out-buildings.

Martha was the oldest child of William Barrow III and his wife, Pheraby. Born in 1809, it was she, with her husband Daniel Turnbull, who built Rosedown in 1834, six years after their marriage in 1828. The house at Rosedown, with its wide, two-storied front galleries, is believed to have been patterned on Martha's birthplace and early home, Highland.

Like her mother before her, Martha created her own lavish gardens as the setting for her new home, importing plants and statuary from Europe, laying out winding walkways, building quaint summerhouses, and planting an avenue of live oak trees leading to the house. Martha so loved her gardens that it is said she was working in them two weeks before her death in 1896, when she was eighty-seven.

It is interesting to note the wide-spread influence that Martha's immediate family had on the plantation culture of the region during these years. Martha's brother, William Ruffin Barrow, built Greenwood, one of the most spectacular Greek Revival mansions in the South. Located only a few miles from Highland and Rosedown, the house burned in 1960. Martha's uncle, Bartholomew Barrow, established the plantation at Afton Villa, still noted for its magnificent gardens. Other Barrow relatives lived at Live Oak, Solitaire, Rosale, Rosebank, Ellerslie, and Wyoming.

Martha and Daniel had three children: James, who died of yellow fever when he was seven; William, who drowned at the age of

Four generations of the Rosedown family are shown in this remarkable photograph taken sometime in the early 1890s. Front row left to right: Rosina Bowman, Martha Bowman Fort holding her young son William Fort III, Martha Turnbull and Corrie Bowman. Back row left to right: George K. Shotwell (husband of Eliza Bowman), Isabel Bowman, Sarah Bowman, Sarah Turnbull Bowman, and James Pirrie Bowman. Martha Turnbull, the matriarch of the family, died in 1896. Her daughter Sarah and son-in-law James P. Bowman eventually inherited Rosedown; their daughter Martha was the first wife of William J. Fort Jr. of nearby Catalpa. The four unmarried Bowman daughters—Isabel, Sarah, Rosina, and Corrie—became the legendary "Bowman Ladies" who held on to their family home during the lean years of the Depression and saved Rosedown for the future.

twenty-seven, leaving a widow and two young sons; and Sarah, who became the eventual heir and mistress of Rosedown. Sarah and her husband, James Bowman of nearby Oakley Plantation, produced ten children. Two of these children were destined to marry into the Fort family of Catalpa Plantation, a mile or so north of Rosedown.

Catalpa was established by the Fort family, who tradition says came to Louisiana in 1800 with their cousins, the Barrows. It was William Fort who built the first house at Catalpa, and his son, William Johnston Fort, who developed the plantation in the 1840s with his wife, Sallie. Together, they turned their home into a show-place set in the midst of a magnificent park. The original house, which reportedly dated from 1800, was a raised cottage with front and back galleries. The gardens contained a picturesque, winding driveway leading to the house, lined with live oak trees and bordered with conch shells. There was an artificial lake, an iron fountain depicting plunging horses, two pigeon houses, a huge deer park, and a magnificent greenhouse. Later a new bride joined the Fort family. She was twenty-two-year-old Martha Bowman, daughter of Sarah and James Bowman of Rosedown. She married William Johnston Fort Jr. in 1880 and lived at Beechwood, another Fort family residence, with him for the next eighteen years. They had two children, Martha and William. Martha Bowman Fort died in 1898 at the age of forty.

Two years later, her widower married his sister-in-law, Mary Bowman of Rosedown, who was thirty-three. This was not an unusual occurrence among plantation families, who often married cousins as well as sisters-in-law and brothers-in-law. Mary Bowman moved to Catalpa and, like her sister Martha, produced two children, Sadie and Mamie. Also like her sister, she was married to William J. Fort Jr. for eighteen years, until his death in 1918.

The original house at Catalpa was destroyed by fire in 1898 or 1899. It was replaced soon thereafter by the present house. It is now a comfortable, high-ceilinged house with a wide center hallway and a deep front gallery. The house is built on the site of the original house, and two cast-iron English greyhounds flank the front steps just as they did when the original house stood.

The Civil War brought hard times to Rosedown and Catalpa, just as it did to other plantations throughout the South. Rosedown was invaded by federal troops, who camped in Martha's gardens, looted the house, stole all the livestock, and burned the crops and numerous outbuildings. At Catalpa, soldiers tore down gates and fences, allowing the cattle to roam freely and destroy much of the old garden. The greenhouse was ruined as well. Although the old driveway and lake are still there, the pigeon houses are gone, as well as the elegant fountain.

By the 1920s and 1930s, the Depression brought more hard times and near-poverty to many formerly-wealthy families in the region. At Rosedown, three of the unmarried Bowman daughters—Miss Sarah, Miss Rosina, and Miss Isabel—became legendary in the region for devoting their lives to the maintenance and preservation of their family home, holding on in spite of seemingly impossible odds. When the last sister, Rosina, died in 1955, she left Rosedown to her nieces and nephews debt-free.

It was in 1956, after 120 years of unbroken family occupancy, that Rosedown was sold. The new owners, Catherine and Milton Underwood of Houston, Texas, undertook an eight-year, $11-million restoration of the property, opening it to the public full-time in 1964. The Underwood's thirty-eight-year tenure at Rosedown was a glory period for the property. Thousands of visitors from all over the world flocked through its gates to visit the mansion and stroll through its lush gardens. After his parents' deaths, the Underwood's son David held on to Rosedown until 1994, when he sold the property to a private individual. In the next seven years much of the original acreage, along with some prized furniture, was sold. At one point, the house was closed to visitors, allowing them access only to the gardens.

Before the property was sold to the State of Louisiana in November of 2000, many other Rosedown artifacts were sold at public auctions or removed, including portraits of Martha and Daniel Turnbull by

Portrait of Sarah Turnbull by Thomas Sully in the front parlor at Catalpa Plantation.

Thomas Sully, and all the original nineteenth-century Italian statues from the gardens.

Rosedown, now a state historic site, is maintained by a staff that includes a full-time site manager, a horticulturalist, a curator of the house, interpretive rangers, maintenance personnel, and tour guides. Open to the public once again, its future seems bright and promising.

Catalpa, like Rosedown, survived the lean years of the Depression, but unlike Rosedown, has remained in the hands of descendants of the original family. Until her death a few years ago, Mrs. Mamie Fort Thompson, great-granddaughter of Martha and Daniel Turnbull and direct descendant of the original William Fort of Catalpa, was something of a legend in her own right. "Miss Mamie" was famous for her wonderful tours of her home whenever visitors came to call. Today, her daughter Mary owns and occupies Catalpa, cherishing her home's history, its various relics of both Rosedown and Catalpa, and its long tradition of hospitality and charm.

Among those relics at Catalpa were the receipts in this cookbook, hand-written by the ladies of Rosedown and Catalpa so long ago and now a permanent part of the histories of these two fascinating Southern plantations.

Stella Pitts

Plantation Cooking in the Antebellum South:
Its Origins and Traditions

"Our tables were filled with every species of meat and vegetable to be found on a plantation, with every kind of cake, jellies, and blanc-mange to be concocted out of eggs, butter, and cream, besides an endless catalogue of preserves, sweetmeats, pickles, and condiments . . . "
—Letitia M. Burwell, *A Girl's Life in Virginia Before the War,* 1895

Throughout the existing literature chronicling the antebellum South—the journals, the letters, the diaries, the travelogues, the novels, and the stories—one aspect of plantation life is nearly always recalled with enthusiasm: the food.

Visitors to the South's fabled plantations, as well as the plantation families themselves, penned detailed and mouth-watering descriptions of the daily meals. They began with the first meal of the plantation day, a hearty breakfast, which usually included several hot meats—fried chicken, fried squirrel, baked hams, and grilled sausages—served with numerous hot breads, including biscuits, spoon bread, muffins, flannel cakes, and rice waffles. Also on the breakfast tables were fresh fruits, jams, jellies, and preserves.

All of this was meant to keep the diners satisfied until the main plantation meal of the day, which was nearly always served between two and four o'clock in the afternoon.

This main meal revealed plantation cooking at its most abundant and delicious. There were rich soups—oyster stews, seafood gumbos, and bisques—and succulent salads of fresh greens, vegetables, and seafoods. Then came the meats—hams, chickens, turkeys, roast beef; many varieties of local game birds like quail, dove, and duck; and fresh fish that was baked, broiled, or stewed.

A wide assortment of vegetables from the plantation gardens filled the porcelain dishes on the tables—green peas and snap beans, turnips and tomatoes, sweet and Irish potatoes, carrots and squash, and eggplant, okra, and cucumbers.

Corn, the South's most basic staple, appeared on the plantation tables in a variety of delicious dishes—fresh on the cob, creamed in puddings, in fritters known as corn oysters, and, of course, in breads, including corn cakes, hoe cakes, corn sticks, corn pone, spoon bread, hominy bread, and crackling bread.

Rice was another Southern staple and nearly always included in plantation dinners—in jambalayas and "hopping john," with gumbos and stews and soups, and served by itself with thick gravies and vegetable sauces.

And always there were hot breads—beaten biscuits, sweet muffins, and fresh-baked loaves dripping with butter.

Then came the desserts, and plantation memoirs seem to glow with fond descriptions of these: coconut cakes and blanc-manges, blackberry cobblers and plum puddings, trifles and custards, tarts and meringues, fruit pies and ice creams, brandied peaches and pears.

Understandably, plantation suppers were light, often simple meals of tea served with biscuits, cold meats, and small cakes.

Inevitably, the origins of Southern cuisine follow the path of Southern history. As one writer put it, "Planted in the seventeenth century, plantation society took root throughout the South in the eighteenth century and flowered in the nineteenth. . . . American cookery and hospitality reached a peak which has seldom if ever been surpassed."

Pilgrims who flocked to the New World in the seventeenth century brought their culinary traditions with them—not only from England,

An original Rosedown Plantation dessert service on the dining room table at Catalpa Plantation.

Scotland, and Ireland, but also from Germany, France, Spain, and Russia. Later on, as their children and grandchildren moved from their original homesteads to the unspoiled wildernesses further South, they found mild climates and lush lands that produced abundant crops, making it possible for many of these new Southerners to build lives of wealth and elegance.

Rural life in the early South, wrote one historian, was "less hurried, less prosaically equalitarian, less futile, richer in picturesqueness, festivity, in realized pleasure that reeked not of hope or fear or unrejoicing labor." And, he added, it was full of good things to eat and drink.

In this rural plantation society, agriculture was the basis of the flourishing economy—cotton, sugar cane, tobacco, rice, and, for a while, indigo. As they grew wealthier, Southerners bought more land,

planted more crops, accrued more wealth, built larger houses. and
established plantations and family dynasties.

And, inevitably, to supply the labor for this plantation economy,
Southerners imported slaves from Africa and the Caribbean Islands.
In doing so, they brought to Southern plantation cuisine one of its
greatest and most lasting influences—that of the unique culinary traditions of the African slave.

Ranked at the top of the plantations' slave hierarchies, the slave
cooks worked under the direction of their mistresses, cooking the
meals they were ordered to cook. Gradually, however, they began to
add their own native touches—certain spices and vegetables and
methods of their own, which were reminders of the homes they had
been forced to leave behind forever. These unique methods have
become the basis of today's Southern cuisine.

In *Southern Food—at Home, on the Road, in History,* author John
Egerton proclaimed that "in the most desolate and hopeless of circumstances, blacks caught in the grip of slavery often exhibited
uncommon wisdom, beauty, strength, and creativity. The kitchen
was one of the few places where their imagination and skill could
have free reign and full expression, and there they often excelled.
From the elegant breads and meats and sweets of plantation cookery
to the inventive genius of Creole cuisine, from beaten biscuits to
bouillabaisse, their legacy of culinary excellence is all the more
impressive considering the extremely adverse conditions in which it
was compiled."

Numerous foodstuffs familiar to us today were probably indigenous
to Africa before European influence—rice, turnips, eggplants, okra,
garlic, and peas, to name only a very few. Cooking techniques in West
Africa used today in this country included steaming in leaves, frying
in deep oil, toasting before the fire, and roasting in the fire itself.

African slaves brought with them to this continent such food
preparation techniques as using okra as a thickener, using smoked
ingredients for flavoring, creating various types of "fritters," and

using rice as the basic ingredient of many dishes. One of the culinary traditions of slaves that is believed to have been imported from the Caribbean Islands, which remains enormously popular today, was barbecued meat.

As a result of these African and Caribbean culinary influences, traditional plantation cuisine in America became a unique blend— the heritage and traditions of the plantation owners "spiced up" by the African cooks.

The plantation kitchen became, of course, a center of continuous activity and life. These kitchens, whether simple frame buildings or elaborate brick structures, were always located a safe distance from the plantation mansion. The reasons were simple—the danger of fire, the excessive heat from the blazing fire always kept burning in the huge fireplaces, and the smells of the cooking that continued from early in the morning until late in the evening.

The slave cooks were often formidable figures, with several underlings to assist them and numerous small children, black and white, running in and out in search of treats.

Simple cast-iron implements were used—kettles, waffle and wafer irons, gridirons, toasters, hanging griddles, frying pans, roasters and long-handled forks and spoons. Once prepared, the dishes were carried into the main house beneath tin covers, arranged on porcelain platters and in tureens and bowls, and carried into the dining room. The elaborate and delicious meals produced in these primitive plantation kitchens with these simple utensils can scarcely be imagined by modern cooks who rely on frozen foods and microwave ovens.

They must return to the volumes of plantation memoirs and search out the descriptions of the meals and food, memories that are eloquent, sometimes amusing and always fascinating.

In 1822, young John Quitman, a native of New York who studied law in Ohio and then settled in Natchez, Mississippi, wrote to his father about a New Year's Day visit to The Forest, a plantation near Natchez.

Inside the Rosedown kitchen cupboard. On the lower left is an original warming bell.

On the table we had green peas, lettuce, radishes, artichokes, new potatoes, and spinach, grown in the open air, and roses, jassamines, jonquils, and pinks in profusion . . . the peach and plum are in full bloom . . .

This enthusiastic New Yorker-turned-Southerner later became a state legislator, a brigadier general in the Mexican War, and governor of Mississippi.

One of many European visitors who toured the South to study its culture and society and then write about it was the English novelist and political economist Harriet Martineau. In 1834, she visited numerous Southern plantations. She left this description of one meal she enjoyed:

> The dinner is plentiful, including, of course, turkey, ham, and sweet potatoes, excellent claret, and large blocks of ice cream. A slave makes a gentle war against the flies with an enormous bunch of peacock feathers, and agitation of the air is pleasant, while the ladies are engaged in eating, so that they cannot use their own fans, which are hung by loops on the backs of their chairs.

In 1833, Henry Bernard, a twenty-two-year-old native of Connecticut and a recent graduate of Yale College, traveled south, visiting a college classmate in Charleston, South Carolina. Young Henry wrote his family about a meal he enjoyed at the home of his friend's family:

> His father served up a grand dinner to a small party—first came a calves head stew as soup—then fish fried or boiled—roast veal, and ducks, with Irish and sweet potatoes—boiled rice (an article of which you can form no opinion from what we ordinarily meet with in the North) and fine bread—peas and beets—turnips and salad. Then came the dessert—another fruit—fine large oranges—pineapple—plantain and bananas (tropical fruits which I have never seen at the North but which resemble richest pear in flavor)—apples—raisins and almonds—prunes and ground nuts and to wash down the whole of each the finest claret, sherry and

madeira wine. We adjourned a little after seven after taking a good cup of coffee.

On festive occasions like Christmas and New Year's and for special events like weddings and christening parties, the plantation kitchen became a swirl of activity, and the cook called in many extra hands to help prepare the food. Letitia M. Burwell recorded this delightful description of an old-fashioned plantation wedding in antebellum Virginia:

> The preparations usually commenced some time before, with saving eggs, butter, chickens, etc., after which ensued the liveliest egg-beating, butter-creaming, raisin-stoning, sugar-pounding, cake-icing, salad-chopping, cocoanut-grating, lemon-squeezing, egg-frothing, waffle-making, pastry-baking, jelly-straining, silver-cleaning, floor-rubbing, dress-making, hair-curling, lace-washing, ruffle-crimping, tarlatan-smoothing, trunk-moving-guests arriving, servants running, girls laughing . . .

In 1853, after an eight-year courtship, young Sara Hicks of Albany, New York, married Benjamin Franklin Williams, a well-to-do North Carolina planter, and moved with him to his family's plantation, Clifton Grove. She wrote her parents many letters describing her new life, which she found quite lively and very different from what she had been used to in the North. In one letter she told of the meals:

> They live more heartily. There must always be two or three different kinds of meats on Mrs. Williams' table for breakfast and dinner. Red pepper is much used to flavor meat with the famous 'barbecue' of the South and which I believe they esteem above all dishes is roasted pig dressed with red pepper and vinegar. Their bread is corn bread, just meal wet with water and without yeast or saleratus, and biscuit with shortening and without anything to make them light and beaten like crackers. The bread and biscuit is always brought to the table hot . . . . I wish we could send you some of our beautiful sweet potatoes and yams.

And, finally, there is this: A description of an oyster roast on Edisto Island, South Carolina, during Christmas celebrations in the 1850s. The writer is I. Jenkins Mikell, whose family had lived on the island since before 1686.

> No sooner had the guests retired to the beach than a rapidly driven wagon came up with the dinner from the home kitchen, packed in extemporized 'fireless cookers,' so that it lost none of its heat, none of its savor. Lucullus [a wealthy Roman consul famous for his banquets] had nothing on it in the way of a feast. True, we did not have nightingale's tongues, but we had, to offset these, diamond-backed terrapin, which was much more sensible. And we had what I know he did not have—palmetto cabbage . . . It has the combined taste of cauliflower, burr artichoke and asparagus, with a most fascinating taste of its own. Lucullus doubtless had an orchestra. Ours was the sighing of the wind through the moss-bearded oaks; the ceaseless chatter of the palmetto fronds, the soft booming of the surf one hundred yards away, interspersed with the frequent high staccato pop of a champagne cork.

This legendary, idyllic, and almost mythical way of life on the Southern plantation disappeared forever in a civil war that many believe was lost the moment the first shot was fired. The plantation economy collapsed when the slaves were freed, planters found themselves penniless and their once-flourishing acres gone to seed, and many of the grand plantation mansions stood empty and desolate.

But, despite ruin and hardship and loss, Southerners held on, retaining many of their finest traditions, among them hospitality, even when there was little to put on their tables except dried peas and corn pone.

And, as they struggled to reclaim their ruined lands, rebuild their homes, and create a new South, Southerners clung to what they had left of the past—the old houses, the family pictures and books and furniture, the bits and pieces remaining of a lost way of life. Among these treasured relics were faded, hand-written recipes penned by

their wives and mothers and grandmothers. They were small but eloquent reminders of the Southern past, tiny but powerful aids in keeping the traditions of Southern cooking alive.

These rare and valuable receipts, like the Turnbull-Bowman
recipes in this cookbook, serve as vivid reminders of a fabled era in
American history that is long past. They also prove that as long as
there are people who delight in Southern cooking—in studying it, in
preparing it, or simply sitting down and eating it—the Southern past
is not dead. In the words of William Faulkner—"it's not even past."

Stella Pitts

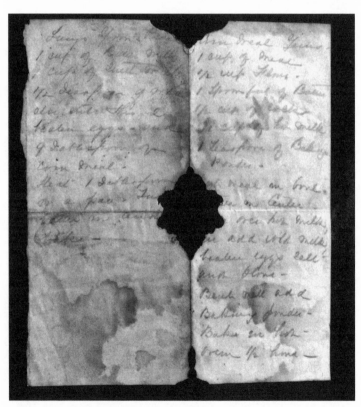

*A hand-written Rosedown receipt for Lucy's Spoon Bread and Corn
Meal Gems.*

Memories of Rosedown

By the time I was old enough to remember visiting my great aunts at Rosedown, they were quite elderly. My mother was close to her mother's family and would visit them often. I was probably four years old when I first remember going with her to Rosedown.

My great aunt Bella always answered the door when we came to call. She was a very slender and frail looking lady but engulfed me in the most powerful hug I've ever had. Even as a little girl, I wondered how this dainty lady had the strength to hug me so hard.

Aunt Nina was the sister who liked being outside. She could usually be found tending to plants or feeding the ducks and geese. Aunt Bella and Aunt Sadie had bedrooms upstairs but Aunt Nina's bedroom was downstairs in the back wing of the house opening to the back porch. This gave her easy access to the outdoors that she loved.

Aunt Sadie was confined to bed by the time I remember her. My mother would take me up to her room to sing my nursery school songs, and I remember her sweet smile as she patiently listened. Before I was born, Aunt Sadie was the sister who conducted tours of the plantation. She evidently established real relationships with many of the tourists who came to Rosedown and exchanged lengthy letters with them for years after.

Aunt Nina and Bella were always very neatly and sedately dressed, even when they were doing chores or working in the garden. Their dresses were usually dark with long sleeves and delicate lace

Rosina (Nina) Bowman.

collars—not really out of date but rather old fashioned looking, even to my childish eyes.

By the time I visited Rosedown, my great-aunts' early lifestyle had been greatly scaled down. Their meals were very simple. The cook, Charlotte, still using the outside kitchen and iron stove, would fix their midday meal, which was the main meal of the day. In the evening, they usually had just tea and toast.

I never had a chance to sample one of the famous Rosedown dinners. Rather than eating, my time at Rosedown was spent playing in the gardens if the weather was warm. Most often I played alone. Sometimes my cousins Martha and Laura, who spent summer vacations at Catalpa, would accompany me. Exploring the overgrown garden paths was a great adventure. The gardens were so large that, to a small child, it was a challenge just not to get lost. In the front garden near the house was a life size cast iron statue of an English setter. It was great fun to climb on his back and to pretend to take a ride down the oak avenue.

One of my favorite outside activities was to have tea parties in the summerhouse with my dolls. I have today the little miniature set of Blue Willow china that Aunt Nina would pack in a small basket for me to take outside to be filled with berries, flower petals and acorns. They say that smells bring back memories more than any of the other senses. I rarely smell sweet olive without remembering the gardens at Rosedown.

In the winter my mother and my great aunts would sit in front of a roaring fire in the dining room and visit. Although my great aunts never left Rosedown and appeared to be very isolated from the outside world, they were in fact, extremely well informed about current events. Each evening they listened to the radio and kept up completely with national and world-wide news.

While they, with my mother, discussed local happenings and global events, I would spend cold days in the library looking at the large volume of McKenny and Hall Indian prints. The wonderful color portraits of Indian chiefs portrayed with painted faces, feather headdresses and bright beads were fascinating to me and I could stay absorbed in them for hours.

My mother's memories of Rosedown visits were, of course, quite different. Both of her grandparents and many of her aunts were alive when she was a child. She would go with her mother and sister every week for Sunday dinner. They would travel from Catalpa to Rosedown by carriage. The ten-minute trip by car today would take about an hour by carriage.

The dinners were very formal and would last from two o'clock until five o'clock. My mother was an active child and normally would have preferred running outside, playing in the creek or riding horseback to sitting politely at a table for three hours. She always said, however, that the food was so good she didn't mind. The meal consisted of seven courses, beginning with oyster gumbo. This would be followed by salad, red fish, turkey, vegetables, a wonderful dessert, and coffee.

My mother's grandmother, Sarah Turnbull, was the disciplinarian and thought that teaching a child good manners was very important. She believed that it was good etiquette to leave a small amount of food on one's plate rather than scraping the plate clean. She told her grandchildren they must always leave a little food on their plate for "Mr. Manners." For years, my mother thought Mr. Manners was a poor starving gardener. She was so mad when she realized she had left all of that wonderful food over the years for a man who didn't exist. My mother's grandfather, James Bowman, presided over the table, carving the large turkeys and roasts. My mother adored him. She thought he was the sweetest grandfather in the world, with his long white beard, kindly brown eyes and, usually a dog at his heels.

When four generations of family were gathered around the dinner table, there was a great sense of connection and love uniting them. Family was the center of their existence and their love of family was embedded in their home. Each object told a story, each room held a memory. It was quite a sacrifice for my great aunts over the years to keep their home completely intact and not part with anything, which

The Rosedown dining room with its original table, chairs, clock, and punkah.

during difficult times would certainly have made their lives easier. When Rosedown was initially sold, virtually nothing had been removed from the house in approximately 150 years.

Since that time, however, major changes have occurred at Rosedown. Fortunately, most of these have been positive ones. The house has been restored to its original splendor. The overgrown gardens that I played in as a child now look as they did when Martha Turnbull designed and planted them in the mid-1800s. Some of the objects, which over the years were removed, are now finding their way back home.

My favorite story is one about my great aunt Corrie's dog collar. Aunt Corrie was the sister who especially loved animals. Some years after she died, Aunt Nina was burning a pile of trash in the back yard. Aunt Sadie, at this time, was conducting tours of the house. A little boy, whose parents were inside having a tour, wandered into the back yard and picked up a dog collar that had fallen out of the trash pile. Aunt Nina told him he could have it. Recently, an elderly gentleman came to tour Rosedown. At the end of the tour, he pulled a dog collar out of his pocket to return to Rosedown. The collar had the names "Corrie" and "Duke" engraved on the silver plate.

In addition to stories like this, many people have purchased and donated back to Rosedown items sold at an auction held before the state bought Rosedown. For those of us with family ties to Rosedown, this is a comforting feeling.

Rosedown is now in safe hands and will be protected in years to come. I think Aunt Bella, Aunt Sadie, and Aunt Nina would be pleased.

Mary Thompson

A Note on the Text

The following receipts have been transcribed from the original manuscripts exactly as they were written with only minor changes. Occasional misspellings were corrected, punctuation has been added where necessary for easier reading, and obscure terms have been defined.

With the exception of the receipts written by Mamie Fort Thompson of Catalpa, most were done by several of the Bowman sisters, by Martha Turnbull, and one by Sarah Turnbull Bowman at Rosedown Plantation. Although most of the receipts were written down between the 1870s and the 1920s, many date from the earliest years of the nineteenth century. Some of these were handed-down family receipts, others were their neighbors' receipts, and some were from present or past cooks. Some of these were influenced by the periodicals, newspapers, and cookbooks of the nineteenth and early twentieth centuries. The ladies had the good habit of recording which newspaper or periodical a receipt was copied. None of the receipts designated as being copied from periodicals and newspapers were used in this work.

Modern readers will observe that many of these early receipts list only ingredients with no further instructions. It should be remembered that most early cooks were expected to know what to do with receipts—they seldom needed detailed directions. However, a number of the receipts in this book do include instructions that can be useful for all.

Conversion Tables

Weights and Measurements

Butter: When soft, one pound is one quart.

Eggs: Ten are one pound.

Wheat Flour: One pound is one quart.

Indian Meal: One pound, two ounces is one quart.

Brown Sugar: One pound, two ounces is one quart.

Sugar Loaf, broken: One pound is one quart.

White Sugar: One pound one ounce is one quart.

Powdered Sugar: One pound, one ounce is one quart.

Flour: Four quarts are half a peck. Sixteen quarts are half a bushel.

Liquids

Four tablespoons are half a gill.

Eight tablespoons are one gill.

Two gills, or sixteen tablespoons, are half a pint.

Two pints are one quart.

Four quarts are one gallon.

Twenty-five drops are one teaspoon.

Four tablespoons are one wineglass.

Twelve tablespoonfuls are one teacup.

Sixteen tablespoonfuls, or half a pint, are one tumbler or coffee cup.

Oven Temperature

Slow oven: 275-300 degrees
Moderate oven: 325-350 degrees
Hot or quick oven: 425-450 degrees

SOUPS

Celery Soup.

Steam the liquor from a
qt of oysters. to then add
strongly water to make
3 qts. Clean & cut into small
pieces the white part of
four bunches of Celery.
Boil the Celery in the
oyster water until it has
boiled [?] days. Let it [?] boil
well, then add a cup full
of flour smoothly blended
with one cup of sweet milk
boil up two or three minutes
salt & pepper to taste. The
[soup] should be about as
thick [as] [?]. If it
should [become] too thick a
[little more] a little more
milk or milk & flour may be
added to bring it to the right
[consistency].

Receipt for Celery Soup (Bowman Family).

LEFT-OVER TURKEY GUMBO
(Bowman Family)

Make a roux with lard or turkey fat & flour, cook in this one table-spoon of minced onion. Add 2 qts of water & the turkey bones. Boil ten minutes, then add 2 dozen oysters, salt, pepper to taste, a ¼ cup of chopped parsley & onion tops. Boil 3 minutes longer, then when ready to serve add while boiling hot 1 tablespoon or more of Gumbo File.

MOCK TURTLE SOUP
(Bowman Family)

Boil the meat in the water to be used as soup if fresh meat is used. Then take out, chop in small pieces & fry well with lard. Make a rich soup & add a can of tomatoes, season with salt & pepper. To 2½ qts of soup add a dessert spoonful of allspice, a teaspoon of cloves, the parsley, thyme, & onion in the soup while boiling. Brown some flour & add an onion chopped fine & also claret to taste.

CELERY SOUP
(Bowman Family)

Strain the liquor from a quart of oysters. To this add enough water to make 3 qts. Clean & cut into small pieces the white portions of three bunches of celery. Boil the celery in the oyster water until it has boiled to [soup]. Let it boil well, then add a cup of flour smoothly blended with one cup of sweet milk. Boil up two or three times & salt & pepper to taste. The [soup] should be about as thick as rich cream. If it should become too thick or too thin in boiling, a little more milk or milk & flour may be added to bring it to the right consistency.

Miss Clevel's Receipts—Irish Potato Soup
(Martha Turnbull)

Select 8 large, firm potatoes, boil until done in the skins, peel &
mash to a paste without lumps with two spoonfuls of butter, pepper &
salt to taste. Return [potatoes] to the soup pot, add ⅔ of a tureen of hot
water, a minced onion, & a slice of bacon. Boil until half reduced,
then add one pint or 1½ pints of hot boiled milk. Pour over toasted
bread & serve instantly.

Directions for making bread: At one o'clock, dissolve in a teacup
of milk-warm water one yeast cake. At sunset sift five pints of flour.
Rub in well a heaping spoonful of lard, add two or three large spoonfuls white sugar, a spoonful of salt, & pour in the dissolved yeast
cake. In cold weather mix the dough with warm water; in summer
make with cold water. The dough must not be too stiff, but stiff
enough to knead well, which do thoroughly. Let it rise all night. Early
the next morning knead again long & well; success depends upon it.
Make into rolls or loaves, let them rise till quite light, & bake in a
well-regulated oven.

Potato Soup
(Mamie Fort Thompson)

½ cup sliced onion
2 tablespoon butter
3 cups thinly sliced potato
2 cups chicken broth
1½ teaspoon salt
1½ cups milk

Smais Potato Soup
(Bowman Family)

Peel & slice very thin four good-sized potatoes. Pour over them 2 cups boiling water & simmer gently till the potatoes are dissolved. Add salt, onions, a lump of butter, & a pint of sweet milk with a dust of pepper. Let it boil up once & serve. Add celery tops if desired.

Calve's Head Soup
(Bowman Family)

1 calve's head skinned
1 set of feet-well cleaned

Boil tender. Take out the bones. Cut fine. Add some sweet marjorum, cloves, black pepper. About 15 minutes before taking up add some small dumplings. If it is too thin, add a little flour & butter thickening. When done, have ready 2 hard-boiled eggs cut fine, 1 teacup wine, & a lemon sliced. Pour over & serve.

SALADS, RELISHES, AND DRESSINGS

To prepare a dainty "Pond Lily Salad," boil hard as many eggs as plates of Salad are desired; then arrange on each plate crisp green lettuce leaves. Cut the whites of the eggs in long thin slices pointed at the ends & broadening towards the center to imitate the petals of the water lily, & arrange them on the lettuce in the cup shape of the flower; then pass the hard yolks through a sieve & heap it in the center; pass dressing with the Salad

Receipt for Pond Lily Salad (Bowman Family).

Salad
(Bowman Family)

One of the prettiest lunch salads is made by cutting the top from green peppers. Remove the seed and fill the pocket with chicken or lobster salad. Each pepper may be placed on a lettuce leaf & covered with a spoonful of mayonnaise.

To prepare a dainty "pond lily salad"
(Bowman Family)

Boil hard as many eggs as plates of salad are desired, then arrange on each plate crisp green lettuce leaves. Cut the whites of the eggs in long thin slices pointed at the ends & broadening towards the center to imitate the petals of the water lily, & arrange them on the lettuce in the cup shape of the flower. Then press the hard yolks through a sieve & heap it in the center. Pass dressing with the salad.

A Pretty salad
(Bowman Family)

Can be made by cutting hearts from cold-boiled beets. Put on crisp lettuce leaves with dabs of mayonnaise dressing. Place slices of hard-boiled eggs around the side of plate.

Celery Salad
(Bowman Family)

Mince the celery very fine. Take one or more boiled eggs, according to the amount of dressing required, while still hot [and] mash thoroughly with a fork until white & yolks are well blended. Add a tablespoon of olive oil or a teaspoon of butter for each egg. When a smooth creamy sauce is formed season with pepper, salt, and vinegar. Pour over cold minced celery or pile the [required] amount of celery on its bed of yellow mayonnaise dressing in the center of a white lettuce leaf and garnish with tiny cubes of tender boiled carrots or beets cut in little stars or cubes. Shape with vegetable cutters.

Thanksgiving Relish
(Bowman Family)

1 can of asparagus tips, 3 hard boiled eggs, ½ cup of vinegar, 2 tablespoons of olive oil, 2 green bell pepper, 1 teaspoon of dry mustard, salt & pepper, 1 head of lettuce. Take 1 large can of asparagus, place 3 tips on saucers. Run through 3 rings of bell pepper resting on 2 or three lettuce leaves. Over this pour a sauce made of yolks of eggs mashed & mixed with dry mustard, olive oil, vinegar, salt & pepper. Ornament the top with chopped white of egg and parsley.

MRS. TOWN'S TOMATOE CATSUP
(Martha Turnbull)

One gallon tomattoe
One quart vinegar
4 tablespoonful Black Pepper
4 do. salt—4 do. mustard
8 pods of green pepper
2 onions
2 garlic

First boil the tomattoe. Pass through a fine sieve, then measure the juice. Flavor according to above directions, boil down to one-half, add cloves, ginger-mace to suit your own taste, 1 tablespoon of whiskey or Brandy. Put in bottles & cork very tight.

TOMATO CATSUP
(Bowman Family)

Put ½ bushel on fire simmer until skin cracks. Pass through a sieve every part but skin and seed. To 6 qts pulp add 3 tablespoon salt, 1 do. ground cloves, 1 do. Allspice, 1 teaspoon red pepper, 1 of black pepper, 3 onions cut fine. Simmer for 2 hours, then cold bottle in small bottles, adding 1 spoon mace or celery seed if liked.

Chow Chow

(Bowman Family)

½ pk Onions, ¼ pk green tomatoes, 1 small pt red and green peppers mixed, 100 small cucumbers. Put over them 1 pt salt; next evening drain well. Add 1 oz white pepper, 1 of mace, 1 of celery seed, ½ oz cloves, 1 oz white and black mustard seed each, 1 jar French mustard, 1½ lb brown sugar, 1 piece horse radish scraped. Cover these with vinegar (leaving out mustard) and put over the fire. When cooled 10 minutes take out the cucumbers, throw them in cold water to crisp them. Let the other ingredients boil ¾ hour. Put the cucumbers in a jar, adding the French mustard and one jar of Blackwells Cauliflower. Pour the boiling pickles over these. Stir all together. When cold add 1 pint olive oil.

Tomatoe Soy

(Bowman Family)

1 peck of green tomatoes, 1 doz onions slice with layers of salt. Let stand 24 hours, drain well, cover with vinegar, and boil until tender. Drain again and cool. Mix 1 lb brown sugar,1 tablespoon black pepper, 1 or 2 oz peel, mace, Cloves, ginger, ½ lb of celery seed, 1 lb of white and ½ lb black mustard seed. Put these ingredients into 1 qt or more of vinegar [and] boil a few minutes. Pour over the tomatoes when cold; add more vinegar if necessary. Then mix a small jar of mustard with one teacup of oil and put on the top. Tie up close.

SALAD DRESSING LIKE MRS. BURTONS

(Bowman Family)

Beat 2 eggs (yolks) light then whip gradually into them 1 cup of vinegar, 2 teaspoonful salt, spoonful mustard, 2 small teaspoonful of white sugar, & paprika & salt to taste. Put into an Agate pot & stir until the boil is reached, when a teaspoonful of butter may be added. Cook still stirring until this melts, then remove from the fire. When cold add olive oil until it is very stiff.

SALAD DRESSING

(Bowman Family)

1 dessert spoon salt (level)
3 tablespoons sugar (rounding)
2 teaspoons mustard (rounding)
1 tablespoon flour (heaping)
4 yolks eggs
3 tablespoons melted butter
1½ cup milk (water is good)
½ cup vinegar (heated)

Mix dry ingredients. Add eggs (beaten), butter, milk or water. Heat all together and then add heated vinegar slowly. Cook in double boiler, or over slow fire until it thickens, stirring all the time. If it should lump beat with egg beater hard—it will become smooth. Cool & use. It will keep a long time in a glass jar (sealed tight—put in a cool place).

A SALAD SANDWICH
(Bowman family)

Is made with a mixture of shredded celery, chopped eggs[and] sliced olives in equal parts, and mayonnaise dressing. This should be spread between thin slices of buttered bread and garnished with sprigs of parsley or celery.

BOILED SALAD DRESSING
(Bowman Family)

½ Teaspoon of salt
1 teaspoon of mustard
1½ Tablespoon of sugar
yolks of two eggs
1½ Tablespoon of melted butter
¼ cup of vinegar
pepper & celery seed if desired

Mix the dry ingredients. Add last of all the eggs which quickly thicken. Cook in a double boiler stirring constantly. When cool, then to the desired courses.

BOILED SALAD DRESSING
(Bowman Family)

Beat the yolks of 2 eggs until smooth. Add ½ teaspoon of mustard, ½ teaspoon salt. Beat in slowly 4 Tablespoons of melted butter, & 3 or 4 of vinegar, ½ teaspoon of sugar. Cook until thick. When cold fold in cream.

MAYONNAISE-SAUCE
(Bowman Family)

Break the yolks of 2 eggs in a deep bowl. Add half a teaspoonful of dry mustard, a little pepper & a salt spoon of salt. In hot weather place the bowl in a saucepan of pounded ice. With a wooden spoon stir these ingredients together & moisten every few minutes, drop by drop with olive oil. After the mixture has been thoroughly worked for a short while add a few drops vinegar, bearing always in mind that the relative qualities of oil & vinegar is five of oil to one drop of vinegar. Impatience will spoil mayonnaise every time.

MAYONNAISE
(Bowman Family)

The yolk of 1 egg, a teaspoon of made mustard, & ½ a teaspoon of salt to be well rubbed together. Pour in very slowly the sweet oil rubbing hard all the time til as much is made as wanted. Then add a tablespoon of vinegar. When these ingredients are mixed they should look perfectly smooth. If it curdles, add a little more mustard or a little vinegar.

EGGLESS MAYONNAISE
(Bowman Family)

To 2 tablespoonful of prepared French mustard beat in ¾ of a teacupful of either olive or Wesson® oil, 1 teaspoonful salt, 1 dessert spoonful sugar, & ½ cupful of thick sweet cream. Stir until well mixed & you will never miss the egg.

Slave-made corn sheller in the Rosedown kitchen. Mid-nineteenth-century, cypress and sheet iron pieces.

BREAD & YEAST

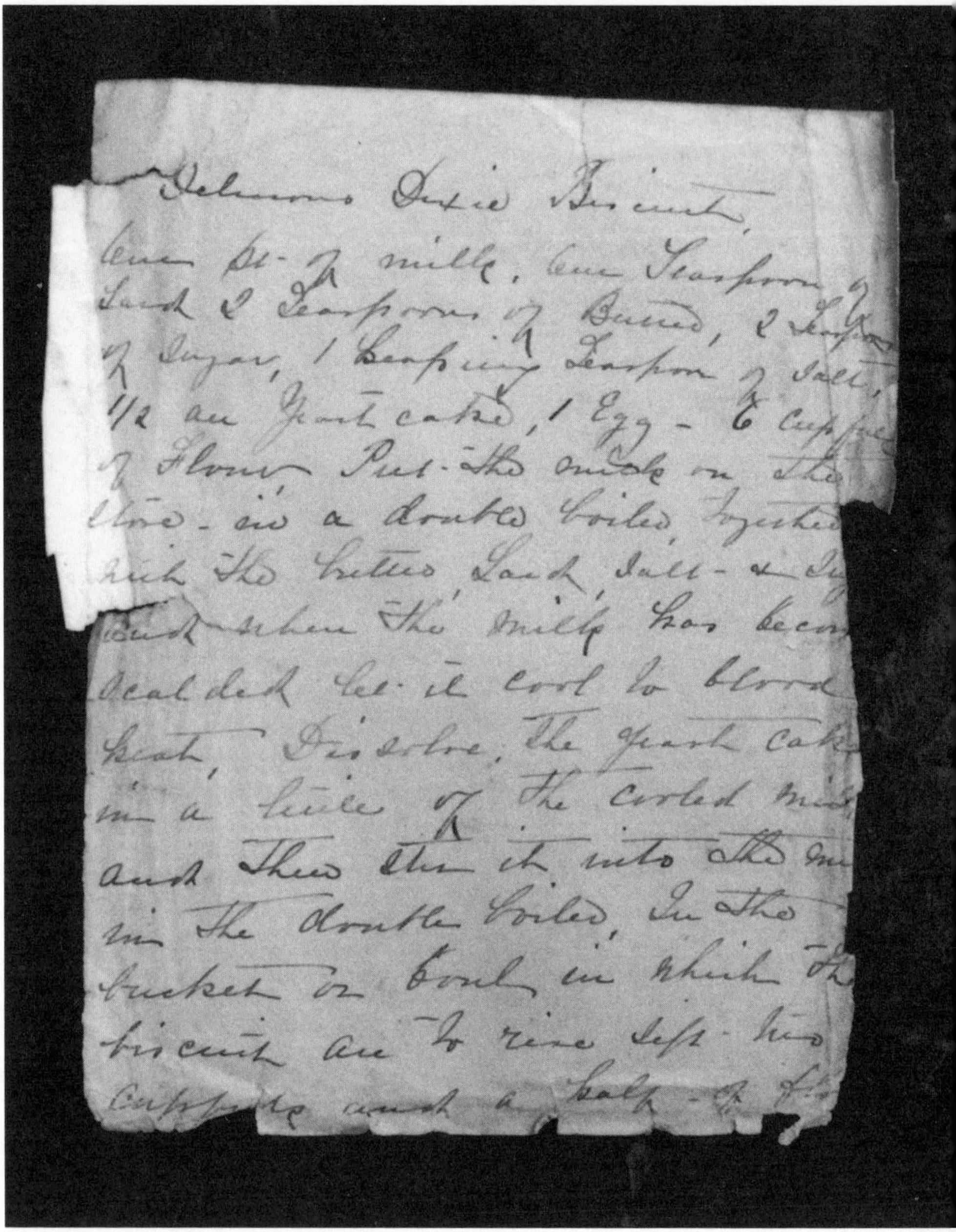

Receipt for Delicious Dixie Biscuits (Bowman family).

BREAD
(Martha Turnbull)

Five pints of flour, 1 tea cup of milk, two of warm water, one table spoonful of sugar, one tea spoonful of salt. Mix with part of the flour to a stiff batter, set it to rise in a warm place (better set the yeast in an earthen pitcher in an oven of warm water & keep hot ashes under the oven so as to keep the water at an even temperature). When it rises well, mix in the remainder of the flour, knead well & bake.

BREAD
(Martha Turnbull)

One teacup of milk, two of warm water, one tablespoonful of sugar, 1 teaspoonful of salt. Mix with a part of the flour to a stiff batter, set it to rise in a warm place, & then add the rest of the flour.

RUSK
(Martha Turnbull)

½ pint of milk warmed, ½ lb of butter, ½ lb of sugar, ½ pint of yeast, or two yeast cakes dissolved in half pint of warm water, 4 eggs, 5 pints of flour. Mix with half the flour, let it rise, mix in remainder of flour, knead half an hour, make into rolls, let it rise again & bake.

HOME MADE BREAD
(Bowman Family)

Put two tablespoons of sugar, two tablespoons of lard, one & one half teaspoon of salt into a mixing bowl. Pour over them two large cups of scalding water or milk. If richer bread is desired, mix one cake of compressed yeast in one-quarter cup of lukewarm water & add to the above mixture. Add gradually six cups of sifted flour to this and stir until smooth. Turn dough on floured board & knead until elastic. Put the dough into a large greased bowl. Cover & let stand over night or about 9 hours in a warm place, in the morning turn out & knead slightly shape into two or three loaves. Place in greased pans & let stand until loaves have doubled in bulk. Bake in hot oven about 30 minutes. Just before taking the bread from the oven rub the crust with melted butter. Remove from oven & from the pans & put in a cool place where air can circulate freely. In cold weather warm the flour slightly before using.

BREAD
(Bowman Family)

5 qt flour, ½ gal water, 1 cup yeast, 2 tablespoon salt. Then knead until quite stiff and leave to rise until morning. Rolls may be made in a similar way with the addition of lard.

MILK YEAST LIGHT BREAD
(Bowman Family)

To one cup of sweet milk add two cups of boiling water, one table-spoon of sugar. Let same cool to blood heat then add 1 teacup of corn meal & 2 cups of flour, stirring same until well mixed. Set in a warm place to rise, stirring every hour for 3 hours. It usually rises in 4 or 5 hrs. Then mix with flour tablespoon of lard & salt to taste set dough to rise in a warm place after dough has risen bake for two hours in a moderate hot stove.

DIRECTIONS FOR MAKING BREAD BY DR BROOKS, LUPHLIN'S YEAST GEMS
(Bowman Family)

Dissolve one of the gems in a pint of warm (not hot) water. Add one teaspoon of salt (one teaspoon of sugar improves it), stir in sufficient flour to make a thin batter and set it to rise in a warm place. In two or three hours stir it thoroughly with two pints of warm water or milk and sufficient flour to make it into a thick batter, cover it with a cloth. In cold weather set it to rise at 7 o'clock in a warm place and keep it warm during the night. In the morning make a stiff dough. Knead it for half an hour then put it in a warm place to rise again. When light mold into small loaves, allow them to stand a short time for further rising and bake in a moderate hot oven. Or, it may be used as any other dry hop yeast. A little warm water rubbed over bread or biscuit will give them a nice color.

Smai's Rice Bread
(Bowman Family)

½ pt of Flour
2 Eggs
½ Cup Boiled Rice
Milk to make a stiff Batter
1 Teaspoon of Butter
1 Teaspoon of Cream Tarter
½ Teaspoon of soda

Rye Bread
(Bowman Family)

Pour two cupfuls of scalded milk over 2 tablespoons each of sugar &
butter, 1 teaspoon of salt. When lukewarm add 1 yeast cake dissolved
in a cup of lukewarm water & six cupfuls of rye flour. Toss on a slightly floured board and knead in 1½ cupfuls of wheat flour. Cover well
& let rise until light & double the bulk. Shape into loaves and put
into greased pans. Cover again let rise & bake.

Mary Rumbles Bread
(Bowman Family)

At 1 o'clock dissolve in a teacup of warm water 1 yeast cake. At sunset sift 5 pts of flour, rub in well a heaping tablespoonful of lard, add
2 or 3 large spoonfuls of salt & pour in the dissolved yeast cake. The
dough must not be too stiff but stiff enough to knead well, which do
thoroughly. Set to rise all night. Early the next morning knead again
long and well. Shape into rolls & set to rise again Bake in a well reg-
ulated stove.

MAMIE'S RECEIPT GINGERBREAD SOFT
(Bowman Family)

1 cup of butter, 1¼ of molasses, 1 cup of sugar, 1 cup of sour milk, 1 teaspoonful of soda dissolved in boiling water, 1 teaspoonful cinnamon, enough ginger to taste, little nutmeg, 3 eggs, 4½ cups of flour. Stir butter, sugar, molasses together, also spice to a tight cream, set on boiler & let get slightly warm, beat the eggs light, add the milk to the warmed mixture, then the eggs, the soda, & lastly the flour, adding a little at a time. Then beat all hard together.

SOUR MILK GINGERBREAD
(Bowman Family)

⅓ cup of butter
1 Egg
½ cup sugar
¾ cup molasses
¾ cup sour milk
1 teaspoon of soda
½ teaspoon of salt
1 teaspoon of Baking Powder
2 cups of flour
Spices

Directions
Cream butter, add sugar, gradually add egg well beaten, then molasses. Mix and sift together the soda, salt, spices, baking powder, and flour. Add alternately with sour milk & beat until smooth, bake in greased pan in moderate oven 45 to 50 minutes.

Southern Spicy Gingerbread
(Bowman Family)

2 eggs, ¾ cup brown sugar, ¾ cup molasses, ¾ cup melted shortening, 2 teaspoons soda, ½ cinnamon, ½ teaspoon cloves, ½ teaspoon nutmeg, ½ teaspoon baking powder, 1 cup boiling water. Add beaten eggs to the sugar, molasses, & melted butter. Then add the dry ingredients, which have been mixed well & sifted, lastly add the boiling water. Bake in shallow pans in moderate oven 30 or 40 minutes.

Delicious Dixie Biscuits
(Bowman Family)

One pt of milk, 1 Teaspoon of lard, 2 Teaspoons of Butter, 2 teaspoons of sugar, 1 heaping Teaspoon of salt, ½ yeast cake, 1 egg, 6 cupfuls of flour. Put the milk on the stove in a double boiler, together with the butter, lard, salt & sugar and when the milk has been scalded let it cool to blood heat. Disolve the yeast cake in a little of the cooled milk and then stir it into the milk in the double boiler. In the bucket or bowl in which the biscuits are to rise, sift two cupfuls and a half of flour. Mix to a stiff batter with the milk which has been prepared. Beat the egg light and add it to the mixture, then beat the batter and keep beating it as for a cake, for the more you beat the better will the biscuit be. Scrape the batter from around the sides of the bucket & cover closely, let the batter rise in a warm place, stir 6 o'clock, then put the batter to rise at 10 AM. At three in the afternoon have the mound of sifted flour, remaining from measure,—on the bread board about 3 cupfuls—& knead as for ordinary biscuit, then double top & [illegible] light. Then roll out to ½ an inch-cut with a small cutter. Brush each biscuit with melted butter, put two together, & brush top with butter & lard. Be careful they do not touch each other. Set them in a warm place cover to let rise until they are twice their size. It will take 2 hours. Bake from 15 to 20 minutes in a hot oven. They are delicious when properly made.

MILK BISCUIT
(Bowman Family)

2 qt flour, 1 pt milk, ½ teaspoon soda, Desert spoon salt, Lump of butter, and lard size of an egg.

COMMON SENSE IN THE HOUSEHOLD—BY MARION HARLAND—MISS E. BISCUIT
(Martha Turnbull)

1 Quart flour, 2 heaping tablespoonfuls of lard, 2 Cups sweet milk, if you can get it new milk, 1 teaspoonful soda, 2 teaspoonful cream tartar, 1 saltspoon of salt

MARYLAND BEATEN BISCUITS
(Bowman Family)

1 qt of Flour, ¼ cup lard, ½ teaspoon salt, 1 cup cold water. Rub the lard & salt into the flour & mix with cold water to a very stiff dough. Knead ten minutes or more until well mixed then beat hard with a biscuit beater or rolling pin, turn the mass over & over until it begins to blister & looks light & puffy, or until pulling off a piece quickly it will give you a sharp snapping sound. When in this condition pull off a small piece, form it into a round biscuit, then pinch off a bit from the top. Turn over & press with the thumb leaving a hollow in center. Prick with a fork. Bake twenty minutes in a quick oven. Butter can be used in place of lard & milk a substitute for water in same proportions.

Carrie Barrow's Biscuit Recipe
(Bowman Family)

1 pt flour
1 small tablespoonful lard
1 teaspoonful soda
1 teaspoonful cream tartar
sour milk to make a soft dough
sweet milk biscuit
½ teaspoonful soda
½ teaspoonful cream tartar

Smai's Soda Biscuit
(Bowman Family)

1 pt Flour
1 Tablespoon of Lard
½ Teaspoon of soda
½ Cup of stiff Clabber

Clabber Biscuit
(Bowman Family)

1 qt of Flour, 6 Tablespoons of melted lard, 2 Teaspoons of Baking Powder, ½ Teaspoon of soda, 1 Teaspoon of salt, Clabber to make a soft dough

Directions
Sift dry ingredients together, add lard and clabber. Cold lumpy clabber makes a stiff hard dough instead of a soft spongy one. In this the clabber is finely divided. Mix all as quickly as possible with the tips of finger, then shape on a floured board & cut. Put immediately into a moderately hot oven and bake quickly about fifteen minutes.

RAISED BISCUIT
(Bowman Family)

1 qt of flour
½ pt new milk or warm water
¼ cup of lard & butter mixed
¼ cup of yeast
1 teaspoon of salt

Put flour in mixing pan, make a hole in center, pour in the milk, add shortening, salt, then yeast, add a little more flour, stir with the hand. Leave to rise until morning then add ½ teaspoon soda & if needed flour to make a stiff dough mold in loaf. Let rise 30 minutes, roll almost ½ inch thick, & cut with biscuit cutter. Put in pan to rise again, rub top & sides with melted butter, when light set in oven to bake.

GINGER BISCUIT
(Bowman Family)

Mix together 1 cupful of molasses with 1 cupful of sour cream, 1 teaspoon of soda, 1 teaspoon of ginger, and one well beaten egg. Add enough flour to make a Biscuit dough. Roll out ½ an inch thick and cut out with a biscuit cutter. Serve hot with coffee.

SWEET POTATOE BISCUIT
(Bowman Family)

1 cup of boiled & finely mashed sweet potatoes, 2 eggs well beaten, 2 cups of flour, 2 teaspoonful B. P., 1 tablespoonful sugar, & 2 cups of milk, 1 tablespoonful butter. Mix together all the dry ingredients & stir into the milk, beaten egg, & potatoes. If too soft add more. Roll out like biscuit.

PUFFS
(Bowman Family)

½ pt water
4 oz scant lard or butter
4 oz of flour good weight
5 eggs
Pinch of salt

Boil the water with the lard or butter & salt in it. Put in the flour all at once & stir the mixture over the fire about five minutes or til it becomes a smooth cooked paste. Then take it off and beat in the eggs one at the time. Drop on buttered tins & bake in moderate oven. Put eggs in while paste is hot & beat hard against the side of the pan.

CHEESE STRAWS
(Bowman Family)

1 cup of grated cheese, lump of butter the size of an egg, 1 cup of unsifted flour, 1 good pinch of cayenne pepper. Mix and knead as biscuit dough. Roll out into a thin dough and cut in strips. Bake in a moderately hot oven.

SMAI'S CORN BREAD
(Bowman Family)

1 qt of meal
2 tablespoons of lard
3½ cups of milk
3 eggs
1 teaspoon of soda
2 teaspoon cream tartar

CRACKLING CORN BREAD
(Bowman Family)

Put 4 cupfuls of corn meal into a mixing Bowl. Add 2 Teaspoons full of salt & 2 Teaspoons of baking powder. Pour over this enough boiling water to moisten. Add 2 cupfuls of crackling. Mix well, pour into a well greased baking pan & bake in hot oven.

VIRGINIA SOFT CORN BREAD
(Bowman Family)

Pour a pt of boiling water over half a pt of corn meal. Add a teaspoonful of salt and let it stand on the back of the stove well covered for a few minutes. Then stir in a tablespoon of butter or lard. One tablespoon of sugar, one well beaten egg, ½ a cupful of milk, and a teaspoonful of baking powder. Beat well & pour into a buttered pudding dish. Bake for at least 30 minutes and serve it in the dish in which it is baked with butter & syrup.

LUCY'S SPOON BREAD
(Bowman Family)

1 cup of butter milk
1 cup of sweet milk
½ teaspoon of soda
stir into this 2 beaten eggs
9 tablespoon of corn meal

Heat 1 tablespoon lard in a pan. Turn batter in and bake.

CORN MEAL GEMS
(Bowman Family)

1 cup of meal
½ cup Flour
1 spoonful of Butter
½ cup of cold [milk]
½ cup of hot milk
1 teaspoon of Baking Powder

Put meal in bowl, Butter in center. Pour over hot milk, then add cold milk, beaten eggs, salt, and flour. Beat well, add Baking powder. Bake in hot oven ½ hour.

FANNIE WILLIAMS ROLLS
(Bowman Family)

½ cup of warm fresh milk
1 Teaspoon of Butter
1 Teaspoon of Lard
1 Tablespoon of sugar
1 well beaten small Egg
¼ teaspoon of salt
¼ cup lukewarm water

Directions
Heat the milk until it steams. Add sugar, Lard & Butter & salt. When cool add ¾ yeast cake dissolved in the ¼ cup water & well beaten egg. Beat this mixture well. Add sufficient flour for soft Biscuit dough, which can be rolled out. Set in a warm place to rise for 2 or 3 hours. Roll out & cut let rise again. Bake in quick oven.

MUFFINS
(Bowman Family)

Two teacups of flour, 3 tablespoonfuls of soft boiled rice (not necessary but better with the rice), Half teaspoonful soda, clabber enough
to make a stiff batter, Two eggs, 1 teaspoon of butter or lard. Beat the
yolks, clabber, soda, & salt together (I suppose you put them into the
flour when well beaten). While beating have the rings heating in or
on the stove. Beat the two whites to a stiff froth with a grain of salt &
three drops of cold water. Pour in the whites & beat until entirely
mixed with the batter, then pour immediately into the pans or it will
fall. If you haven't sour milk use sweet and one teaspoonful Cream
Tartar to ½ soda.

Amelia says if you can't get them right she will have to come over
some morning & show you again.

RAISED MUFFINS
(Bowman Family)

One tumblerful of raised dough, three eggs, three tablespoonsful of
butter, half a cup of white sugar. The dough must be taken after the
bread has passed the second rising. Work in the butter first then the
eggs and the sugar beaten together until very light. Bake about twenty
minutes in muffin rings.

Rice Muffins good

(Bowman Family)

Mash a Cupful of cold boiled Rice. Add 1½ tablespoonfuls of melted butter and the yolks of two eggs well beaten, one cup of cold milk, one teaspoon of salt, gradually add 1½ cupful of flour. Beat the mixture well, stir in the beaten whites, then add 2 level teaspoonfuls of baking powder. Mix light. Bake in a moderately hot oven 20 minutes.

Miss Lucie Buster's Potatoe Yeast Receipt

(Bowman Family)

Take one qt potatoes, boil them with the peelings left on, add a good handful of hops. Put in a muslin bag, all boiled in 2 qts of water until they are done, then mash potatoes up real fine & when milk warm add a cup of yeast, a cup of sugar, & a cup of salt. When it has risen, which will be in about 24 hours, then strain through a colander, then set in a cool place & when making bread use 2 cups of water to one cup of yeast.

Amelia's good Yeast cakes

(Bowman Family)

3 Yeast cakes dissolved for half an hour in milk warm water. Add it to ¾ pint of flour, then the hop tea (drawn from a hand full of hops as you draw tea), then add about one and a half tablespoonful of brown sugar and in summer a pinch of soda. Let this rise in summer about four hours in winter over night near the fire. Then add two pints of meal or more if not thick enough, cut in cakes, and dry in the shade.

FRITTERS, ETC.

An excellent recipe for
Corn Fritters

Select 3 Large ears filled
under [...] of Corn —
Cut twice very thinly then
Scrape out the balance
of pulp — Beat [...] 2
eggs until very light
and add [...] Corn —
Thicken with flour until
of a consistency that will
fall easily from the spoon
[...] 1 cup of milk and
[...] to taste
No baking powder is
required for this receipt.
The secret of success is
not to have the batter too
thick or stiff — and not
too thin — Drop the
batter from a large

Receipt for corn fritters (Bowman Family).

FRITTERS
(Bowman Family)

1 scoop of flour, 5 eggs, 1 cup of dry boiled rice and mashed fine, 1 teaspoon salt. Let it cool, and add alternately part of milk and flour beating well. Batter same stiffness as muffins, fry as doughnuts.

FRITTERS MRS MONTAGUE
(Bowman Family)

Two hours before dinner, boil 1 pt of water with a piece of butter [the] size of a walnut and the rind of a lemon. Sift 1 pt of flour and mix with enough water to blend it, then pour over it the boiling water. Return it to the fire and boil for a few minutes, then spread it on a dish to cool. When perfectly cool, beat in 4 eggs one at a time and put away to rise. Have nearly 1 pint of boiling lard and drop in in small quantities. Fry [until] brown.

Sauce ¼ lb of butter creamed with 6 large tablespoons of sugar, 1 egg beaten light, ½ nutmeg, 1 glass wine. Let it come to a scald and let it cool. The batter must be thick enough to drop from a spoon.

RICE CROQUETTES
(Bowman Family)

Two cups of cold boiled rice, 1 well-beaten egg, 1 teaspoon butter, 1 teaspoon sugar, salt to taste. Work the butter and all into the rice. Make into croquettes with floured hands & fry in lard.

An Excellent Recipe for Corn Fritters
(Bowman Family)

Select three large, well-filled, tender ears of corn. Cut twice very thinly then scrape out the balance of pulp. Beat well 2 eggs until very light and add to corn. Thicken with flour until of a consistency that will fall easily from the spoon. Add one cup of milk and salt to taste.

No baking powder is required for this receipt. The secret of success is not to have the batter too thick or stiff and not too thin. Drop the batter from a large spoon into boiling lard.

Canned Corn Fritters
(Bowman Family)

Empty the contents of a can of corn into a colander. Run cold water over it to rinse off the liquid in which it is cooked and thus rid of tinny taste. Chop the corn fine, mix with two cupful of this, a cupful of milk to which you have added a pinch of soda, a teaspoon of melted butter, 2 well beaten eggs, 2 tablespoonfuls of flour, a little sugar, & salt. Drop by the spoonful into boiling fat. Fry until brown.

DELICIOUS APPLE FRITTERS
(Bowman Family)

2 apples
1 cup of flour
1½ teaspoon of baking powder
3 tablespoons of powdered sugar
¼ teaspoon of salt
⅓ cup of milk
1 Egg

Sift the flour with the baking powder and salt into a bowl. Add sugar and gradually add the milk, lastly add the egg well beaten. Core & cut the apples in slices, dip in batter, and fry in deep fat to a delicate brown, then take them out and drain on some brown paper. Sprinkle with sugar & cinnamon, serve hot.

STUFFED APPLES (GOOD)
(Bowman Family)

Peel apples, core them, and drop in boiling water. Cook until tender, let get cool, & fill with chopped raisins, almonds, or pecans. Put in pan [and] serve cold with either cream or hard sauce.

Sauce
Whip the whites of 2 eggs to a stiff froth, cream 1 cup of butter with 1½ cups of sugar. Stir in the whites flavor with 1 teaspoon vanilla or 1 wine glass of sherry wine.

Baked Pears
(Bowman Family)

Take five large cooking pears. Peel, core, & split lengthwise. Place in a shallow pan, sprinkle with 1½ cup of sugar. Sprinkle with water—enough in pan to cover the bottom—& a tablespoon of butter. Place in an oven to bake. When partly tender, fill the cavities with equal portions of raisins & pecans, basting occasionally. Brown underneath the glaze & serve cold with whipped cream. The pears are also nice to cook as above described & when removed from the stove to fill cavities with red or white cherries & serve.

VEGETABLES

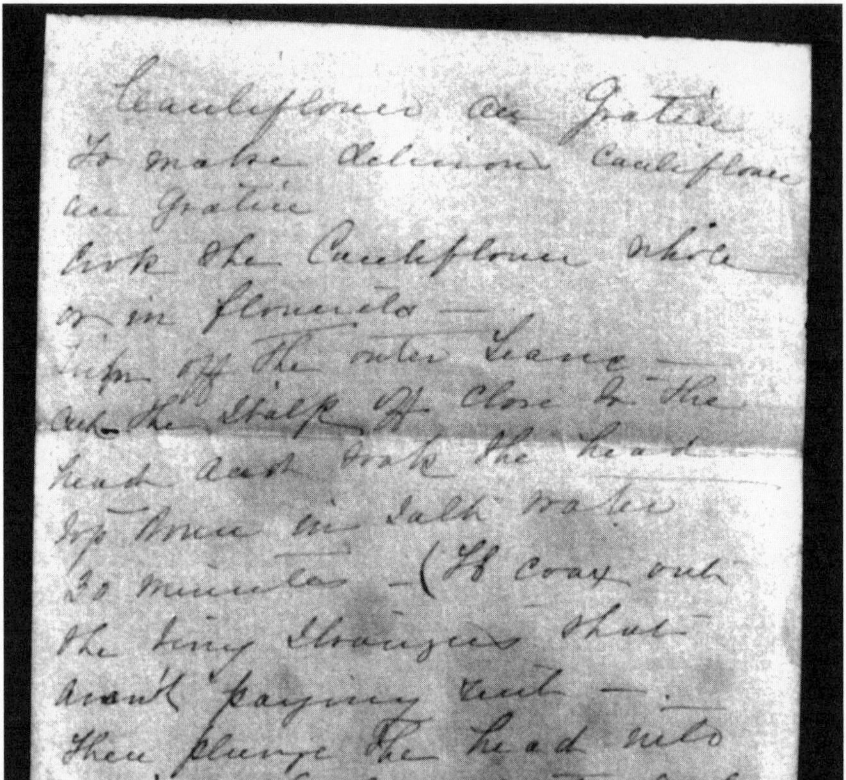

Receipt for Cauliflower au Gratin (Bowman Family).

Stuffed Cabbage
(Bowman Family)

Trim a cabbage to the point when all the leaves are perfect. Then lay back from the center of the cabbage the outer leaves, but do not cut them in order to keep it whole. Take a knife and cut out a cavity in the heart of the cabbage sufficiently large to hold 3 cupfuls of stuffing. Take 1 cupful of lean, finely-chopped ham, 1 good-size onion, ½ teaspoon of ground sage, ½ teaspoon of celery salt, 1 teaspoon of chopped parsley, ½ a teaspoonful of pepper, 2 cupfuls of grated bread crumbs, 2 tablespoons of melted butter. These should be well mixed & salted & bound together with gravy or milk. Fill the cavity with this mixture & then cover over the outer leaves of the head. Tie up the head in fresh cheesecloth & drop in a kettle of boiling water that has been salted to taste. Put something in the kettle so the head does not rest on the bottom. This should boil hard in a covered kettle until the cabbage is perfectly tender, then remove from cheesecloth, drain in a colander and set in the hot oven. Serve with drawn butter & pepper sauce. Garnish with cold-boiled sliced eggs or cut length-wise slice from the center to the outer edge.

Stuffed Onions
(Bowman Family)

Choose onions of equal size [and] remove the hearts, making a large hole in the center of each. Cut equal quarters of veal, kidney, and bacon into tiny bits and season with pepper & a little mixed herbs. Fill into the centers of the onions and replace the tops, holding them firm with skewers. Put into a baking pan with a generous quantity of butter & bake in a moderate oven until thoroughly cooked. Baste with butter & serve on hot toast with a meat course.

BAKED STUFFED ONIONS
(Bowman Family)

6 large onions
1 tablespoon of minced pepper
1 tablespoon melted butter
4 tablespoons of hot water
½ cup of buttered coarse bread crumbs
salt and red pepper

Parboil onions for 10 minutes in enough boiling salted water to cover. Scoop out the center of onion. Place upside down on a platter to drain. Saute the chopped mixture in melted butter. Fill onions with this mixture. Place in a pan, pour around them hot water, and bake in a moderate oven. Sprinkle grated breadcrumbs on top of each.

CAULIFLOWER
(Bowman Family)

It greatly improves the flavor and appearance of cauliflower to simmer it tender in half milk & half water. Never boil cauliflower with the lid on pot. The liquor which does not boil down may be thickened with butter & flour, after which one has a tasty sauce.

CAULIFLOWER AU GRATIN
(Bowman Family)

To make delicious cauliflower au gratin:
Cook the cauliflower whole or in flowerets. Trim off the outer leaves. Cut the stalk off close to the head and soak the head top down in salt water 30 minutes (to coax out the tiny strangers that aren't paying rent). Then plunge the head into rapidly boiling water and cook uncovered 20 to 30 minutes depending on size. Never let cauliflower cook til it falls apart—it gets murky. Melt 2 tablespoons butter. Slowly blend in 2 tablespoons of flour. Gradually stir in 1 cup of milk & then one cup grated or ground cheese. Add seasoning to taste. Put cauliflower in greased baking dish, pour sauce over top with buttered crumbs, & bake in moderate oven until crumbs are brown. Serve hot.

CAULIFLOWER WITH WHITE SAUCE
(Bowman Family)

Remove the green leaves from the cauliflower and place it top downwards in a dish of cold salt water, then wash & wrap in in a piece of cloth, drop it stem downwards into hot salted water & boil 20 minutes. Lift it out carefully & drain in a warm place. Sauce: cook a tablespoon of butter with an equal quantity of flour but do not let brown. Then add a coffee cup of hot milk, mix smooth, & season with salt & pepper. Sometimes hot-boiled cauliflower is sprinkled with grated cheese & then with buttered cracker or bread crumbs & baked to a light brown.

BAKED SQUASH

(Bowman Family)

Boil several medium-sized squash until tender enough to mash. Drain well the mash through a coarse colander to extract seed. Heat a large spoonful of butter in a frying pan. Brown but do not burn. Add salt & pepper to taste. Mix all with the squash. Put into shells or baking dish, sprinkle breadcrumbs on top, & a little butter. Place in oven & brown.

POTATO PIES

(Bowman Family)

4 large potatoes
2 tablespoonful of butter
beat well together until light
8 tablespoonful brown sugar
break two eggs in it and beat well
add half-cup milk (sweet)
put in cinnamon and nutmeg
if you prefer lemon, squeeze in nearly a whole one-
for sweet potatoes as the same way only use-the cinnamon as spice and not lemon

POTATO PONE

(Bowman Family)

Grate 4 large potatoes; the peel of one lemon; 1 teaspoon each of brown sugar, molasses, butter, & milk; 4 eggs; ½ teaspoon nutmeg, cloves, & cinnamon. Beat eggs, butter, & sugar until creamed. Add other ingredients. Put in well buttered pan & bake slowly. Serve cold or hot with sauce.

FISH, ETC.

Receipt for Salmon Loaf (Bowman Family).

91

SALMON BALLS

(Bowman Family)

Pick the bones from a can of salmon and break the meat up with a fork. Add two well-beaten eggs, some fine cracker crumbs, and milk enough to make a stiff batter. Season and mold into balls. Fry in hot butter or lard to a light brown. Serve on a hot platter. Garnish with parsley and lemon.

SALMON CUTLETS OF CANNED SALMON

(Bowman Family)

Open the can [of salmon] some hours before using the contents & turn out the fish. Flake into bits with a silver fork & keep on the ice. Fry a slice of onion in a tablespoonful of butter for a minute, then remove the onion & stir in a tablespoonful flour & cook to a smooth roux. Add slowly a cup of cream & stir until thick and smooth, then beat in the flaked salmon & season with salt, pepper, lemon juice, a dash of nutmeg, & a tablespoonful of minced parsley. As soon as this mixture is heated thoroughly, take from the fire & add the beaten yolks of 2 eggs. Return to the fire for a minute only, then remove. set on the ice until cold and stiff. Form into cutlet shapes. Dip each in cracker dust, then in beaten egg, & again in cracker dust, & set all on a platter on the ice for two hours before frying to a golden brown in deep boiling lard. Serve with tartar sauce.

Salmon Loaf
By Mrs J. L. Creath
(Bowman Family)

Drain the oil from a can of the best salmon & flake the fish. Remove any bones. Heat a tablespoon of butter in a frying pan. In this saute a tablespoon of minced onion. Add the salmon oil, one cup of milk, pepper, salt, dash of tabasco sauce, tablespoon of chopped parsley, & a cup of fine cracker crumbs. Remove pan from fire, add two slightly beaten eggs & the salmon. Mix all thoroughly. Turn into well-greased loaf pan. Bake about three quarters of an hour & turn out with a hot platter. Serve sliced with melted butter to which has been added a little finely chopped onions, parsley, & vinegar pickles.

Salmon Timbales
(Bowman Family)

Flake into small bits enough cold salmon to make a cupful. Cook together in a sauce pan a tablespoonful each of butter and flour. When these are blended, pour upon them one cup of milk. Stir to a smooth sauce, seasoning with salt and pepper and a dash of lemon. Stir in the minced fish & a sprig of parsley, boil for a half minute then remove from the fire. Set aside until cold, then add gradually the yolks of three eggs, and last of all fold in the stiff egg whites. Pour into molds filled ⅔ full. Bake immediately in an outer pan of heated water for twenty minutes. While they are baking prepare a white sauce. Turn the timbales upon a heated dish pour the white sauce around them. Serve at once. Six timbales of medium size may be made from this.

Love is stronger than ambition, consideration for others is better than selfishness.

SIMPLE LUNCH DISH # 2
(Bowman Family)

Make some good-sized baking powder biscuits. Smooth the top over when they go into the oven, then cool. Cut out a round piece in top of each one and take out the crumbs, leaving a shell. Put a little butter inside, spread around the walls, and fill each one with creamed salmon or other fish, heaping it up well in pyramid form. Put an extra spoonful of cream on the top and a sprig of parsley. A dish of pears goes well with these little patties.

FISH SALAD
(Bowman Family)

Take any cooked fish or canned salmon & flake it. Lay on it some mayonnaise or cooked dressing & sprinkle all over with finely chopped pickle or capers. Border with lettuce leaves.

FISH
(Bowman Family)

Fish can be scaled much easier by dipping in boiling water about a minute. Salt fish of any kind is quickest and best freshed by soaking in some milk.

FISH SAUCE
(Bowman Family)

The yolks of 3 eggs, 1 teaspoon vinegar, ¼ lb of butter, a little salt. Stir over a slow fire.

FISH
(Bowman Family)

As a rule, the top of a fish should be garnished with a slice of lemon and a sprig of parsley. Pass dressed cucumbers.

OYSTER COCKTAIL
(Bowman Family)

4 tablespoons of tomato catsup, 1 tablespoon of horseradish, 10 drops of Tobasco® sauce, and the juice of 1 lemon. This makes an excellent sauce for eight portions.

DEVILED OYSTERS
(Bowman Family)

[Deviled Oysters] are prepared by drying & laying them for a while in lemon juice & melted butter seasoned with red pepper. Then dip in breadcrumbs, in beaten eggs, again in crumbs, & fry in deep lard.

THE CREAMED OYSTERS IN TOASTED CUPS
(Bowman Family)

Firm one pint of oysters by pouring one quart of boiling water over them, drain & chop fine. In the chafing dish melt two tablespoonful of butter, turn in the oysters, dust with a little salt and pepper, & saute until nicely browned. Add 2 tablespoonful of powdered crackers & ¾ of a cup of sweet cream. Stir all together & cook 3 minutes. Serve in toast-cups garnished with parsley.

To make the toast-cups, cut slices of bread 2 inches thick & 4 inches square. Remove the crust & scoop out the crumbs until a shell is formed about ½ an inch all around. Brush inside and outside with melted butter & brown in a quick oven.

LOBSTER CROQUETTES
(Bowman Family)

They are a delicate entrée & can be made from canned lobster. Strain off the liquor, and chop in fine pieces, soak one or two slices of bread in water, remove the crust & squeeze dry. Mix well with the lobster, season with salt & pepper. Mix to a paste with a well-beaten egg. Mold into the usual croquette shape. Dip in a beaten egg & then in breadcrumbs & fry in boiling lard.

FOWL

Scalloped Turkey

Butter a baking dish + put in
a layer of bread crumbs, the
cold stuffing over the turkey
moisten the meat a little with
stock — all the turkey scraps of which
put a thick layer on the dish.
Sprinkle with salt pepper —
then cover with _____
lots of butter on top — then
more meat, crumbs, thick the bread
crumbs pour all the left over
gravy on the last layer. Put
another piece of butter and
then cover + bake for half an
hour, more or less —
a couple of beaten eggs may
be added stir a little milk
also used — to make a
richer dish.

Pastry —

1½ cups flour ⅓ cup of lard ¼
cup of water. Salt — ¼ teaspoon of
_____ powder. Sift the flour with
_____ powder in a bowl. Rub in
the lard — make a stiff dough with
ice water — then roll out and _____

fold — let stand five min.
_____ each time let stand a few min.
_____ then bake —

Receipt for Scalloped Turkey (Bowman Family).

BOILED CHICKEN
(Bowman Family)

Draw a chicken & wipe with a wet towel; rub the fowl well with lemon juice. Pin in a piece of cheesecloth. Put the fowl into boiling salted water & allow it to boil slowly, about 20 minutes to each pound of fowl. When it is tender, take it carefully out of the cloth so as not to break the flesh & put in a roasting pan. Place in a hot oven, baste with melted butter until a rich brown, & serve with oyster sauce and cranberry jelly.

CROQUETTES
(Bowman Family)

A cold chicken cut fine, 2 sweet breads parboiled and minced, season with salt, pepper, and parsley chopped fine. Wet the whole with cream or milk to make a paste. Shape with a jelly glass. Line the forms with breadcrumbs. Fry them quickly [until] a light brown.

CHICKEN MOUSSE

(Mamie Fort Thompson)

1 cup stale bread crumbs
1 cup milk
4 tablespoons butter
1 cup chopped cooked chicken
½ teaspoon salt
⅛ teaspoon pepper
2 egg whites beaten stiff

Cook breadcrumbs & milk to smooth paste, add butter, chicken, salt & pepper, then fold in stiffly beaten egg whites. Pour into buttered mold & bake in pan of water on several thicknesses of paper for twenty minutes or until firm. Serve with mushroom sauce.
[For sauce] Cook mushrooms in butter for ten minutes, then sprinkle with flour, add pint of cream.

CHICKEN SANDWICHES

(Bowman Family)

Are made by slicing finger rolls lengthwise & scooping out most of the crumbs & filling the inside half of each with chicken salad. Put on the upper half of the roll & tie together with narrow ribbon using a shade to harmonize with the table decorations.

CHICKEN SALAD
(Bowman Family)

2 large chickens. 1½ bottle sweet oil, 2½ tablespoon mustard. Begin by breaking the yolks of 3 raw eggs into a deep plate. Add the mustard, 1 teaspoon vinegar, a very little oil at a time until all is used. Have ready the yolks of 18 hard-boiled eggs. Mix very lightly into a teacup of vinegar. Stir this dressing into the first a teaspoon at a time.

A dainty little supper can consist of Creamed Oysters in Toast Cups and Chicken Salad. Plates decorated with lettuce leaves.

SCALLOPED TURKEY
(Bowman Family)

Butter a baking dish & put in a layer of breadcrumbs. The cold stuffing will do also—moisten this with a little milk. Take all the small scraps of turkey [and] put a thick layer in the dish. Sprinkle with salt, pepper, celery, and then breadcrumbs with lots of butter on top, then one more meat, finishing with the breadcrumbs. Pour all the left over gravy on the last layer of crumbs [with] plenty of butter and then cover & bake for half an hour, [uncover] and brown.

TURKEY JELLY
(Bowman Family)

You may make a stock from the bones of the turkey. Soak half a box of gelatine in cold water until soft. Season the stock well, cleaning it by boiling it up with the white and shell of an egg & strain. Stir the gelatine in while boiling hot & set it aside to cool. Season well with onion juice, celery, salt, & a little vinegar if liked. Put the jelly in a mold to form with slices of cold turkey in it interspersed with stoned olives [and] sliced hard-boiled egg. When firm, turn on a flat dish with celery decorations.

MEATS &
MEAT SAUCES

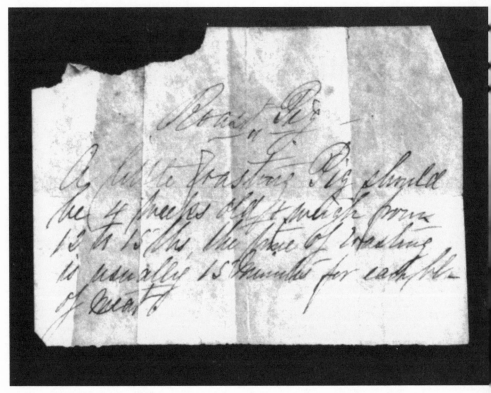

Receipt for Roast Pig (Bowman Family).

Mrs. Wethuill's Meat Croquets
(Bowman Family)

Chop the meat very fine, then mash the potatoes very smooth. Cut an onion fine. Mix these well together, then beat an egg and stir in with a little cream, salt to taste. Form into shape with hands and roll into the yellow of an egg, then in fine breadcrumbs. Fry in hot boiling lard. A little parsley will improve them.

Corned Beef Hash Croquette
(Bowman Family)

Two cups of finely chopped cold corned beef, one tablespoon of chopped parsley, two cups of mashed potatoes, one egg, two tablespoons of butter, one-fourth cup of cream, & salt & pepper to taste.

Melt the butter in a saucepan, add the potatoes & cream & stir until it is well mixed & heated. Add the meat & the salt & pepper. Take from the fire, add chopped parsley & the egg beaten light without separating. Mix well but gently & put away to cool. Form to croquettes. Cover with egg & breadcrumbs & fry in deep smoking hot fat. Serve with sauce.

Roast Pig
(Bowman Family)

A little roasting pig should be 4 weeks old & weigh from 12 to 15 lbs. The time of roasting is usually 15 minutes for each pound of meat.

MINCED HAM ON FRENCH TOAST
(Bowman Family)

To 1 egg well beaten, add ½ cup of milk. Into this dip slices of bread
& fry these in butter. After return the toast to a hot platter and put in
a warm place. Put chopped ham in a small skillet, cover with milk,
and add a small piece of butter. When thoroughly heated, add 1 egg
well beaten. Serve on the slices of toast.

MINCED PORK SANDWICH
(Bowman Family)

⅔ cup of chopped cooked pork
¼ cup chopped sweet pickle
1 hard boiled chopped egg
¼ teaspoon of salt
4 tablespoons of salad dressing

Mix the ingredients and spread on buttered sliced bread. Makes 6.

STUFFED HAM
(Bowman Family)

Soak the ham overnight. In the morning take off the skin. Have ready
equal parts of parsley, sage, & one minced onion, ground allspice,
cloves, black and red pepper to taste, and about fifteen soda crackers rolled fine. Stick a large knife in the ham lengthwise—that is
from the large fat end to the back—& press the knife back until each
hole can be filled with the stuffing. When all the holes are filled, lay
the skin back on the ham & tie tight with cord & bake slowly for
about four hours. When done remove the string and rub meat with
[sugar] and let brown.

BAKED CABBAGE WITH MEAT
(Bowman Family)

Shred one head of cabbage very fine and stand it in cold water 2 hours, then drain thoroughly. Place a layer of the shredded cabbage in a deep baking dish. On it place a layer of cooked meat chopped fine—ham is especially good. Season each layer with butter, salt, pepper a cupful of meat at a time. Sprinkle over the meat a tablespoon of grated cheese. On this place another layer of cabbage & so on until the dish is full, having a layer of the meat with cheese on top. Pour over this a cupful and a half of boiling water and cook covered in a moderate oven 1½ hours. At least half an hour before the dish is served, pour over it a cupful of sweet cream or milk thick and rich with butter. Cover 15 minutes, then remove cover & cook 15 minutes. The top should be a delicate brown.

STEAK
(Bowman Family)

[For] the best sirloin steak, ask the butcher for the "hip Bone sirloin."

BRINE CURED PORK
(Bowman Family)

Rub the meat well with salt, let stand 24 hours to drain out the blood. Prepare a brine for each 100 lbs of meat: 8 lbs of salt, 2 lbs of sugar, 2 oz of saltpeter, 1 oz of red pepper, 4 gallons of hot water. Stir until the ingredients are dissolved. Pack the meat tightly in a barrel using salt in the bottom & between the layers. Pour the well-cooled brine over the meat. Weight down. When the meat has been in the brine a week, overhaul & repack, putting the top pieces in the bottom of the barrel. The meat should be overhauled a second time in ten days. It will cure in from 4 to 6 weeks—it depends upon size of pieces. Take the meat from brine, wipe dry, and smoke.

Corned Beef

(Bowman Family)

To corn 10 lbs of beef:
2 qts of water
1 lb of salt
1 cup of brown sugar
1½ tablespoonfuls of saltpeter pulverized

Boil this in a brine, skim, and then cool. When cold add the beef. Put a heavy weight on the meat and keep well covered. Turn every day and in five or six days it will be ready for use.

Green Tomato Soy

(Bowman Family)

2 gallons tomatoes, green and sliced thin without peeling
2 good-sized onions also sliced
1 quart sugar
2 qts vinegar
2 tablespoons salt
2 tablespoons ground mustard
2 tablespoons black pepper ground
1 tablespoon allspice
1 tablespoon cloves
Mix all together and stew until tender, stirring often so as not to scorch. Put up in small jars. This [is] a most useful and pleasant sauce for almost all kinds of meats and fish.

HADEN SAUCE
(Bowman Family)

1 gal chopped cabbage
2 qts chopped green tomatoes
1 qt chopped onions
½ pt chopped green peppers (hot)
1 tablespoon ground cloves
1 tablespoon ground allspice
2 tablespoon ground cinnamon
1 tablespoon ground mace
1 tablespoon ground black pepper
2 tablespoon celery seed
4 tablespoon mustard seed, white
4 tablespoon mustard seed, black
2 qts vinegar
2 lbs brown sugar
Salt to taste
Boil 2 hours

WINE SAUCE
(Bowman Family)

Beat one cupful of butter until it is creamy. Then gradually heat into it two cupfuls of powdered sugar & when this is done add a gill sherry by spoonfuls. Beat the mixture till it becomes a smooth, light froth, then set the bowl in a basin of boiling water & stir for a minute & a half. Have the sauce bowl heated by means of boiling water. Grate a part of nutmeg over the sauce & send it hot to the table.

EGGS, ETC.

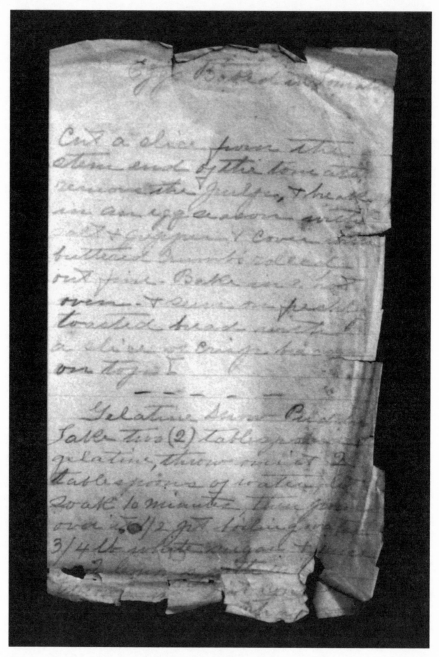

Receipt for Eggs Baked in Tomatoes (Bowman Family).

DAINTY TOAST
(Bowman Family)

Toast a slice of bread and dip into a small quantity of hot water to which has been added a generous piece of butter. Remove from water, pile on top of toast the beaten white of an egg, placing the yolk squarely in the center. Salt slightly, set in hot oven until the egg is firm but not hard.

BREAKFAST SUGGESTIONS
(Bowman Family)

Take stale rolls or large biscuit, first cutting even slices on top. Scoop out the center of each round, leaving a narrow rim and remove the crumbs. Rub the case these formed well with butter, drop an egg in each cavity, sprinkle with salt and pepper. Put in a hot oven till the eggs are set. The shells can be toasted, can be filled with creamed fish. Sprinkle a little parsley on top.

EGGS FOR BREAKFAST
(Bowman Family)

Whip the whites to a stiff froth, then put this into a pan and make small hollows in the whip and drop the yolks into each hollow. Bake this by setting in a pan of hot water until a light brown.

Eggs Baked in Tomatoes
(Bowman Family)

Cut a slice from the stem end of the tomato, remove the pulp, and break in an egg. Season with salt and pepper, and cover with buttered crumbs rolled out fine. Bake in a hot oven, and serve on freshly toasted bread with a slice of crisp bacon on top.

Minced Mutton with Poached Eggs
(Bowman Family)

Chop the mutton very fine. Put two cupfuls of this into a frying-pan with half an onion minced and a half-cupful of good gravy. If you have none, use instead a little hot water and a lump of butter the size of an egg. Just before taking from the fire, stir into a tablespoonful of Worcestershire sauce or two of tomato catsup. Heap the mince on small squares of buttered toast laid on a hot platter and place a poached egg on top. Serve very hot.

Stuffed Eggs
(Bowman Family)

one dozen eggs
one can deviled ham
one half teaspoon, salt, a few drops of tabasco® sauce, and one tablespoon of olive oil.

Hardboil eggs, when cold cut shell lengthwise and remove yolks. Cream the yolks, adding oil gradually. To this add deviled ham, salt, and tabasco sauce. Mix carefully until ingredients are thoroughly blended. Fill the whites of the eggs with the above mixture. A little pickle or olives chopped fine add flavor if desired.

BAKED SPAGHETTI WITH EGGS AND CHEESE
(Bowman Family)

Put the spaghetti in a pan of fast boiling water and cook until tender-then drain. Thickly butter a baking pan, put a thick layer of spaghetti, then slices of hard-boiled eggs. Dust these with pepper and salt. Cover this layer with spaghetti, pour a white sauce over this, then add little lumps of butter and sprinkle with grated cheese. Bake in a quick oven for ten minutes and decorate with sliced egg and chopped parsley.

SARDINE EGGS-MAKE AN APPETIZING SPRING SALAD
(Bowman Family)

Cut hard-boiled eggs lengthwise and remove the yolks, leaving the whites intact. Bone a few sardines; moisten these with a few drops of vinegar. Fill the egg cups with the mixture (yolks and sardines). Place them on lettuce leaves and serve with mayonnaise jelly cut in fancy shapes.

To make the jelly, simply add enough gelatine to an ordinary, highly-seasoned mayonnaise to make it stiff. Good proportions for jelly are one raw yolk of egg beaten smooth with half a cup of olive oil, ⅛ of a teaspoon of mustard, a teaspoon or more of sharp vinegar-salt and pepper to taste, A teaspoon full of gelatine soaked in cold water-then dissolve in three teaspoons of boiling water. Let the gelatine harden in a shallow plate on ice so that it will not be too thick and can cut easily into any shape desired [such as] triangles, stars, etc.

Cheese Toast
(Bowman Family)

Cut thick squares of sliced bread and between each two lay a thick slice of cheese. Dust them with a little cayenne pepper. Put in a hot chafing dish a tablespoon of butter, and when it bubbles lay in the sandwiches. Have ready hot plates and when the cheese has melted and the bread is well browned on both sides, slip one on each plate and serve hot.

Welsh Rarebit
(Bowman Family)

½ lb cheese
½ cup milk
1 tablespoon butter
1 tablespoon corn starch
¼ teaspoon each salt and mustard and a little cayenne pepper

The cornstarch is cooked in the butter, then the milk is gradually added and cooked two minutes. Then the cheese is added until it is melted. Season and serve on crackers or bread toasted on one side, the rarebit being poured on the toasted side.

PUNCHES, ETC.

BEN R. MAYER,
PRESIDENT.

A. O. BARROW,
VICE PRESIDENT.

C. J. BARROW,
SECRETARY, TREASURER
AND GENERAL MANAGER.

Capital Stock $50,000.

Baton Rouge Liquor & Cigar Co. Limited.

Wholesale Dealers in

Foreign and Domestic Wines, Liquors and Cigars.

Corner Lafayette and Florida Streets.

CINCINNATI OFFICE,
211 FRONT ST., CINCINNATI, OHIO.

ESTABLISHED 1893.

Baton Rouge, La., _____ 190___

For the edification of those who
would like to indulge in this
truly bewitching treat the following receipe is furnished.

Highland Punch:

Usy a tall glass put in a few spears
of mint three or four dashes of
orange bitters, one dash of angustura
three or four dashes of gum syrup
or plain fruit syrup and the
juice of half a lemon. Crush these
together, add a wine glass of
apple jack. Then fill glass with
crushed ice and shake well.
Serve and decorate glass with
fruit. Serve with straws.

Receipt for Highland Punch (Bowman Family).

(Bowman Family)

For the edification of those who would like to indulge in this truly bewitching treat the following recipe is furnished.

HIGHLAND PUNCH

Use a tall glass. Put in a few spears of mint, three or four dashes of orange bitters, one dash of angostura, three or four dashes of gum syrup, plain fruit syrup, and the juice of half a lemon. Crush these together, add a wine glass of apple jack, then fill glass with crushed ice and shake well. Serve and decorate glass with fruit. Serve with straws.

FRUIT PUNCH
(Bowman Family)

Put one cupful of water [and] 2 cupfuls of sugar in a stewing pan. Let boil 10 minutes. Add 1 cupful of fresh hot tea, 2 cupfuls of canned strawberry juice, juice of 6 lemons, juice of five oranges, 1 can of grated pineapple. Cover and let stand for ½ hour, then strain. Add ice water to make 1½ gallons of liquid. Just before serving add 1 qt of Apollinaris water & 1 cupful of Maraschino cherries. Turn into a fruit bowl with a large piece of ice.

SYLLABUB
(Bowman Family)

2 glasses of wine
juice of one lemon
1 cup sugar
1 pint of cream

BLACKBERRY WINE
(Bowman Family)

To 1 qt of water, [add] 3 pints of berries. Mash & let stand 24 hours. Strain as jelly. To one gallon of this juice add 2½ lbs of brown sugar, white of an egg beaten to a stiff froth. Put all in a ½ barrel filled up to the brim. Shake every morning, filling it full from a jug of juice kept for the purpose, so it can throw off the impurities as it works. When it has ceased to ferment, which will be in about 2 or 3 weeks, cover tightly & keep in a cool place 3 or 4 months, then draw off carefully & bottle. Put a lump of loaf sugar into each bottle, cork, & seal.

BLACKBERRY CORDIAL
(Bowman Family)

To 1 qt strained juice [add] 1 lb loaf sugar. When dissolved put in a kettle with ½ oz stick cinnamon, ½ oz cloves. Boil to a thick jelly and to every quart add ½ pint of best Brandy, straining first, and bottle. Keep the spice in if preferred.

DOUGHNUTS,
WAFFLES, ETC.

Receipt for Old Auntie's Sweet Wafers (Bowman Family).

Fine Waffles
(Bowman Family)

2 Cups of Flour
1 Heaping teaspoonful of Baking Powder
pinch of salt
3 well beaten eggs
1¼ cups of milk
1 tablespoonful melted butter
Have the Irons well greased & very hot

Waffles
(Bowman Family)

4 eggs, 1 qt milk, 1 lb flour, butter size of an egg, ½ pt yeast.

Waffles
(Bowman Family)

The secret of fine Waffles is to have the irons good and hot. Have a cup of melted Lard or Butter on the stove and a long handled paint Brush to grease them with. Grease the irons well on one side, then turn & grease on the other side.

Receipt
2 Cups of Flour
1 Heaping Teaspoon of Baking Powder
Pinch of salt
3 well beaten eggs
1¼ cups of milk
1 Teaspoon of melted Butter

WAFFLES
(Bowman Family)

1 cup of flour, ½ cup of milk, 1 egg, 2 teaspoon of butter, 1 teaspoon of baking powder

Directions
Sift flour in bucket. Mix in the milk, break the egg in, beating very hard. Pour in the butter after melting. Then ready to bake, add the baking powder. Irons must be very hot. Fire steady.

A DELICIOUS WAFFLE RECIPE
(Bowman Family)

Separate 4 eggs, beat yolks well
Sift 3 cups of flour
4 teaspoons of Baking Powder
½ teaspoon of salt

Directions
To beaten yolks add alternately dry ingredients & 2 cups of milk, ½ cup of melted butter. Fold in beaten whites, mix only long enough to blend thoroughly. Too much beating makes tough.

DOUGHNUTS
(Bowman Family)

1 lb sugar beaten with the whites and yolks of a half a dozen eggs, then pour in one quart of warm milk, two yeast cakes, a piece of butter the size of an egg, 2 qt of flour, one nutmeg. Fry in lard.

Doughnuts (Mrs H)

(Bowman Family)

2 yolks of eggs
1 white of eggs
1½ scant Cupfuls sugar
½ scant Cupfuls butter milk
½ teaspoonful soda
1 tablespoonful butter
nutmeg, cinnamon & salt to taste
enough flour to make a tolerably soft dough

Sour Milk Doughnuts

(Bowman Family)

Add a cup of sugar to one well beaten egg. To this add a cup of some milk into which a scant half teaspoon of soda has been stirred, salt & spices to taste. Mix with enough flour to make a soft dough. A teaspoon of baking powder sifted into the flour gives added lightness. Cut & fry in hot fat. Drain on brown paper & dust with powdered sugar.

Buck Wheat Cakes

(Bowman Family)

Take 2 cups of buck wheat flour, 2 tablespoons of baking powder, ½ teaspoon of salt. Sift well while dry, then mix with sweet milk into a thin batter. Bake at once on a hot griddle.

Corn Meal Griddle Cakes
(Bowman Family)

Three eggs well beaten, a cup of milk stirred into them, teaspoonful of lard melted in a little boiling water. Stir this into a pint of meal. Add eggs and milk. If the batter is not thin enough add more milk or water, and drop two large spoonfull on hot greased griddle. Brown on both sides.

Old Auntie's Sweet Wafers
(Bowman Family)

1 cup of sugar
2 eggs
½ cup sweet milk
Tablespoon ½ butter ½ lard
½ teaspoon of cinnamon

Directions
Beat the sugar & eggs together, then add gradually Flour & milk. Make a thin batter for cake. Roll while hot.

CAKES AND CONFECTIONS

Cup Cake

4 Eggs –
1 Cup butter
2 Sugar
½ Cup milk
3 ½ Cups sifted flour
2 Spoonfuls Yeast Powder

Receipt for Cup Cake (Bowman Family).

SUMMER SPONGE CAKE
(Bowman Family)

Beat the yolks of 2 eggs until frothy, add ¼ cup of strained orange juice and a tablespoon of lemon juice and continue to beat until the mixture is thick & yellow. Add ¾ cup of sugar and a little of the grated orange rind & when well blended add the stiffly beaten whites of the two Eggs. Sift together a cup of flour and a ¼ teaspoon of flour & fold into the first mixture. Pour into a buttered and floured pan and bake in a medium oven for 45 minutes.

SPONGE CAKE GOOD
(Bowman Family)

12 eggs
The weight of the eggs in sugar
Half of this weight in flour
1 lemon juice & rind

Beat yolks & whites very light, the sugar with the yolks, until light & smooth. Next the juice & peel of the lemon, then the beaten whites, lastly the flour very lightly. Bake in a steady oven & cover the cake with paper. Line the pan with paper.

CREAM SPONGE CAKE (MRS H)

(Bowman Family)

2 eggs beaten separately
1 heaping cup of flour
1 cup of granulated sugar
¾ cup sweet cream
1 teaspoonful soda
2 teaspoonful cream tartar
Beat hard & add whites last
Bake in a mold or square pan

ALMOND CREAM CAKE MRS H

(Bowman Family)

10 whites of eggs
1 tumbler of flour
1½ tumbler of pulverized sugar
1 heaping teaspoon cream tartar

Have whites beaten stiff & sprinkle sugar over them, then flour, into which cream tartar has been sifted. Stir gently, but do not beat it. Bake in jelly pans.

For Filling
½ pt sweet cream
Yolks of 3 eggs
1 tablespoon sugar
1 teaspoon corn starch
Flavor with almond

Pecan Cake (Mrs H)

(Bowman Family)

1 lb of New Orleans sugar
1 lb of Flour
⅓ lb of Butter
2 lbs Raisins
2 lbs Pecans before cracking
1 teaspoonful Baking Powder
1 nutmeg
6 eggs beaten separately
1 wine glass of whisky
Put in cake pan & bake about three hours

Lightning Cake

(Bowman Family)

Sift together 1½ cupful of flour, 1 cupful of sugar, & 1 level teaspoonful of baking powder. Into a cup ⅓ filled with melted butter, break 2 eggs & fill the cup with sweet milk, mix, bake, & serve warm. This little receipt never fails.

Cake

(Martha Turnbull)

2 lb flour
½ lb lard
1 lb sugar
5 eggs
1 teaspoonful salaratus [baking soda]

CUP CAKE
(Bowman Family)

4 Eggs
1 cup butter
2 sugar
½ cup milk
3½ cup sifted flour
2 spoonful Yeast Powders

CUP CAKE (MRS H)
(Bowman Family)

5 whites of eggs
¾ cup of butter
1 cup of milk
2 cups of sugar
3 cups of flour sifted three times
2 teaspoons baking powder put in flour

Cream butter, add sugar, then milk & flour, & lastly the whites well beaten. Bake in small mold or muffin ring.

CRUMB CAKES
(Bowman Family)

1 qt milk, eight eggs, 1 pt breadcrumbs, 1 tablespoon salt, lump of butter size of an egg, 2 yeast cakes or half a cup of yeast, 1 qt flour.

MRS WATSON'S CHOCOLATE CAKE
(Bowman Family)

1 cup of butter, 2 cups of sugar, 3 of flour, & 4 eggs, ½ cup sweet milk, 1 teaspoon soda, 2 of cream tartar

Filling
3 cups white sugar with just enough water to cover. Boil until a thick syrup. Into the whites of three eggs, which have been beaten to a stiff froth, [add] 2 teaspoons of vanilla. Then add the grated chocolate, beating constantly.

PEACH SHORT CAKE
(Bowman Family)

Bake a sponge cake in a deep round pan, when cool split in half & lift off the upper half of the cake carefully with a broad knife so it will not break. On the lower portion of the cake put drained & sliced drained canned peaches. Sprinkle thickly with powdered sugar, spread with whipped cream, & replace the upper half of the cake. Heap whipped cream on this.

Strawberry Short Cake
(Bowman Family)

2 pts of flour
½ teacup lard & butter mixed
2 scant teaspoons baking powder
½ teaspoon salt
enough sour milk to slightly mix to handle

Place on the board, divide dough into two parts, roll half almost ¾ of an inch thick & place on buttered tin. With a knife, spread over this portion a little melted butter. Roll remainder of the dough the same size & shape & place on top of the other dough, put in hot oven & bake a chestnut brown. Take 1 qt of strawberries & put in porcelain kettle with one pt of granulated sugar & a little cold water to moisten. Stir until done. When the cake is done remove from tin & place on a plate, separate the layers. Put upper one inverted over another plate & butter well the two surfaces. Fill the lower layer plentifully with strawberries & dredge with powdered sugar. Then place upper layer over crust downwards, press together lightly with the fingers, & fill top inside surface same as lower. Set in a warm place & cover until ready to eat.

NUT & FRUIT CAKE
(Mamie Fort Thompson)

Whites of 4 eggs beaten well
1 C white sugar
½ C butter
½ C sweet milk
1½ C flour
1½ tsp B. P.
½ C pecans chopped fine
¼ C almonds chopped fine
Bake in 2 layers

Dark part
Yolks of 4 eggs
1 C sugar
½ C butter
½ C sweet milk
1½ C flour
1½ tsp B. P.
½ tsp each nutmeg, allspice, cinnamon, ginger & cloves
½ lb seedless raisins cut fine & floured well
Bake in 2 layers

Fruit Cake
(Bowman Family)

12 eggs, 1 lb brown sugar, 1 lb butter, 1 lb of browned flour sifted, 2 lbs of currants washed and dried, 2 lbs raisins seeded and cut, 1 lb citron, 3 nutmegs, 2 teaspoons of mace ground, 1 tablespoon Cinnamon, 1 teaspoon cloves, ½ pint wine and brandy, 1/2 lb almonds blanched and cut fine, ½ pint molasses. Cream butter and sugar very light, add the eggs well beaten alternately with the flour, pour wine in slowly, then the fruit well dredged. Mix well. Grease and paper the pans. Oven heat for Bread.

Mary Butler's White Fruit Cake
(Bowman Family)

1 lb Flour, 1 lb Butter, 1 lb sugar, 14 eggs—whites only, 1 wine glass of Sherry, Mace to taste, 2 lbs of Citron, 2 lbs of Almonds, 1 Cocoanut, flour, all fruit

Sarah, own way of making White Fruit Cake
(Martha Turnbull)

11 Eggs, 2 lbs Cocoanut, 12 oz Butter, 1 lb Flour, 1 lb Citron, 1 lb Almonds, Wineglass of Wine, 1 lb sugar. Cream butter & sugar together, then by degrees add flour & whites of eggs after being well beaten. Add the fruit well mixed & the wine by degrees. Old Minerva took 28 eggs (whites only) for 2 lbs White Cake. For the Cocoanut cake, 2 lbs Butter, 2 Sugar, 2 of Flour, 5 Cocoanuts grated. She baked the batter on the griddle, mixed the cocoanut with the whites of six eggs as for Icing, & sugar in the same way, & spread between each then Cake.

MRS LEWIS' WHITE LEMON CAKE
(Martha Turnbull)

1 & ½ Cups Sugar, ½ Cup butter, 3 Cups Flour, Whites of 3 Eggs, 2 Heaping Teaspoonfuls of yeast Powders.

Dressing: The Yolks of 3 Eggs, 1 Cup Sugar, juice of 2 Lemons. Boil the Peel of Lemons until soft, changing the water to extract the Bitter. Cut up fine, add yolks, Sugar & Juice. Put on fire until boiled thick, stirring to keep from burning, then spread on cake as in jelly cake.

HICKORY NUT CAKE
(Bowman Family)

Beat 1 cup of butter until light & beat into it 2 cups of sugar. Add the yolks of four eggs, the whites beaten to a froth, 1 cup of milk, 3½ cups of flour into which 2 teaspoonful of baking powder has been sifted. Have ready 1 cup of nuts dredged with flour. Mix these into the butter, flavor with almond or lemon & bake in a moderate oven.

Chocolate Layer Cake

(Corrie Bowman)

Dear Virginia

This cake I think you will be proud to serve your guests at your first party. I have given many social affairs, serving this cake each time, which has never failed me & always receiving the highest praise.

Chocolate Layer Cake
½ cupful of Butter
1½ cupful of Fine Granulated Sugar
1 cupful of milk, 3 Eggs
3 small cupful of Pastry Flour
2 Level Teaspoonful Royal Baking Powder
½ Teaspoonful Vanilla

Mash the butter in tepid warm water until soft enough to beat, drain off water & gradually sift in the sugar, with inward strokes (Do not stir but beat). Add the well beaten yolks of eggs, Sift flour & baking powder three times together, then add alternately with milk to the first mixture, add vanilla, & last carefully fold in the well beaten whites of eggs, with as few strokes as possible. Have 4 layer cake pans ready prepared by brushing with butter or Oleo (never lard). Then sprinkle well with flour, shake the pan vigorously then turn over then shake all loose flour from them. Now pour the batter into the 4 pans, tap the pans once or twice. This produces a velvety texture & an even surface. Place in a moderate oven. If your range is operated with gas, oil or electricity, do not light the oven burners until you are ready to put the cake batter into the pans. A coal or wood range must have all the draughts closed & the oven door left ajar for several moments to reduce the temperature (as slow baking is safe baking), gradually increasing the heat as the cake begins to bake. Do not open the oven for at least 10 minutes after the cake goes in. A layer cake baked in a moderate oven will require from 20 to 35 minutes. When thoroughly baked it will shrink from the pans. Turn out & put together with the following Chocolate Icing.

Boiled Icing
3 Cupful granulated sugar
1 Cupful of water
3 Egg whites
2 Tablespoonful with cocoa or grated unsweetened chocolate
½ teaspoonful vanilla, Pinch of cinnamon

Cook the sugar & water slowly without stirring until syrup spins a thread. Sift Chocolate & Cinnamon into well beaten whites of eggs. Then pour boiling syrup over this, beating all the while. Now add vanilla. Beat until thick, Spread between layers & top of cake, while icing is still soft sprinkle with crushed pecans or walnuts & decorate top with halved nuts placed in circles.

Miss Corrie Bowman

"Rosedown Plantation" St. Francisville, Louisiana

Orange Cake
(Bowman Family)

2 cups of sugar, 2 cups of Flour, ½ cup of water, 1 teaspoon of cream
tarter mixed well through the flour, ½ teaspoon of soda dissolved in
the water, whites of 3 eggs beaten to a stiff froth, yolks of 5 eggs well
beaten, Juice and rind of 1 orange. Mix all together and spread on
tins as for jelly cake.

For the inside, beat the whites of 2 eggs to a stiff froth add one
orange that is the juice and rind, and sugar as if for frosting. Insert
this between the layers and frost the top.

Jam Cake
(Bowman Family)

1 cup butter
2 cups sugar
4 cups flour
2 cups jam
½ cup sour cream or buttermilk
1 level teaspoon of soda beaten in cream or milk just as you use-
6 eggs
1 teaspoon cinnamon and one of cloves and one of allspice and a
grating of nutmeg
Mix like any cake, adding jam last.

APPLE CAKE
(Mamie Fort Thompson)

1 egg
1½ Cups sugar
½ Cup of butter
2½ Cups flour
1 Cup raisins
1 Cup chopped nuts
1½ Cups stewed apples
2 Level teaspoons soda and beat the soda into the apples
Spices, cinnamon, all spice, nutmeg & ginger to taste, about ½ teaspoon each
Fine.

WHITE CAKE
(Bowman Family)

Whites of 12 eggs beaten to a stiff froth, ¾ lb of butter, 8 lb of flour, 1 lb sugar, 2 small teaspoons Cream Tarter sifted through flour, 1 small teaspoon soda in a little cream, ½ lb citron cut fine.

WHITE CAKE
(Bowman Family)

One cup of butter, two cups of white sugar. Three heaping cups of unsifted rising flour, the whites only of eight eggs. Flavor with almond. Bake in a slow oven.

Mrs Doherty's White or Brides Cake
(Martha Turnbull)

Whites of 18 Eggs, the weights of 12 Eggs in sugar, weight of 9 eggs in flour, & four of butter. Flavor with almond.

Coffee Cake
(Bowman Family)

4 eggs, 5 oz butter, ½ pt rich milk, ½ lb white sugar, 2 teaspoonful yeast powder rubbed through 1 qt of flour. Consistency of pound cake.

Old Aunty's Flannel Cakes
(Bowman Family)

1 qt of flour, 1½ pt of sour milk, 1 teaspoon of soda, 2 eggs. Sift Flour, pour in milk &, after beating in the two eggs, mix all together, adding salt & soda. Then fry on griddle with plenty of lard.

A Good Cake for Scarce Seasons
(Bowman Family)

One lb & three-quarters of flour sifted. One pound & a quarter of sugar—fair brown will answer perfectly. Three quarters of a lb of butter creamed, one lb & a half of raisins seeded & grated nutmeg, an even teaspoonful of soda & a pt of milk slightly sour, lastly only four well beaten eggs separately. Add the milk & soda last. Bake in a cake mould. This cake is excellent as a pudding with wine sauce, but the better in flavor if kept until the next day & eaten cold. Bake almost two hours. This receipt is large enough for two puddings.

GINGER CAKE (MRS H)
(Bowman Family)

5 eggs beaten separately
2 cups brown sugar
1 cup Molasses, not too dark
3½ cups Flour
1 teaspoonful soda
pinch of Cayenne pepper
1 heaping tablespoonful of ginger
1 dessert spoonful Cinnamon
1 cup sour Cream or butter milk
½ cup butter & lard mixed
Dissolve soda in the butter milk & bake in a long pan.

GINGER CAKE
(Bowman Family)

⅓ cup lard [creamed with] 1 cup sugar
1 egg, not separated but beaten light
1 teaspoon soda dissolved in ½ cup syrup
2 cups flour
nutmeg & cinnamon
Last add boiling water. Put in greased pan & bake.

GINGER POUND CAKE
(Bowman Family)

Take 1 lb of sugar, ½ doz eggs, 1 cup of butter, ½ pt molasses, ½ pt sour milk. Dissolve in the latter ½ teaspoon soda. Beat first the sugar with butter and yolks of eggs well together. Then add molasses milk and soda, 2 tablespoons of ginger, 1 dessert spoon ground Cinnamon, and flavor according to taste either with lemon or vanilla. After having beaten all this together, beat well the whites of eggs and add to it, flour enough to make a pound cake batter, and bake it with slow heat.

SPICE CAKE
(Bowman Family)

2 cups of brown sugar
3 eggs
¼ lb of butter
1 teaspoon of nutmeg
1½ teaspoon of cinnamon
½ teaspoon of cloves
1 cup of sour milk
1 teaspoon of soda dissolved in the milk
2½ cups of flour

Icing
3 tablespoons of melted butter, ¾ lbs of confectioners sugar, enough scalded milk to make icing spread, and 1 teaspoon of vanilla.

DIXIE SPICE CAKE
(Bowman Family)

⅓ Cup of Butter
2 Eggs
2 Cups of sifted Flour
½ Teaspoon of Cinnamon
½ Teaspoon of nutmeg
1⅓ cups of sifted Brown Sugar
½ cup of milk
2½ Teaspoons of Baking Powder
1 cup Chopped Raisins
½ Teaspoon of salt

Directions
Put all ingredients together in bowl and beat thoroughly until smooth. Bake in Loaf pan 20 minutes. Bake as cup cakes [for] 15 minutes. Ice with white or caramel icing.

CAKE ITEMS
(Bowman Family)

When the cake rises way up in the middle you will know the dough was too thick. If it slumps in the center you put in too much sugar and the dough was too thick. If the cake has large holes you used too much baking powder.

CARAMEL ICING
(Bowman Family)

2½ cups of Brown sugar
1¼ cups of Cream
1 tablespoon of butter
1 Teaspoon of vanilla

Cook to a soft Ball shape & beat to the right consistency to spread. Sprinkle with Chopped Pecans.

CHOCOLATE FILLING
(Bowman Family)

1 pt sour milk
½ pt sugar
Yolk of one egg
1 tablespoon Flour pinch of salt
3 squares of Bakers Chocolate

Put milk in sauce pan with Chocolate & half of sugar. Beat yolk & add rest of sugar, & a little cold water, flour, & salt. Stir until smooth when chocolate has dissolved. Add the flour. Stir constantly until it boils & thickens, flavor with Vanilla. When cold spread between layers of cake.

BRANDY FOR CHOCOLATE
(Bowman Family)

Whenever you use chocolate add a drop of brandy; it is the only thing that brings out the real flavor. In making chocolate cake I add a teaspoon of brandy. For icing use a teaspoonful of brandy to each white of egg. Chocolate for drinking purposes needs a teaspoonful of brandy for each 2 cupfuls in the pot. Add it when the liquid is nearly melted. The brandy also helps to bring out the vanilla flavoring, but it is not to be considered a substitute for it.

ORANGE FILLING
(Bowman Family)

Put the juice of three medium sized oranges into a double boiler, add the grated rind of one lemon & the juice of 2 lemons & cook [over] boiling heat. Add 1 cupful of sugar, butter the size of a walnut, & 2 tablespoonfuls of corn starch dissolved in cold waters stirring constantly until smooth & thoroughly cooked. Spread the filling on the cake while warm. Cover the top with white frosting.

COCOANUT FILLING
(Bowman Family)

Make a boiled icing of 2 cups of sugar [and] 2 whites of Eggs

Directions
Boil the sugar until it ropes from spoon, then add this to the two whites which have been beaten to a stiff froth. Continue beating until it gets only warm & stiff, then add sufficient cocoanut to make it thick enough to spread on cake.

Ladies Icing Recipe
(Bowman Family)

½ cup white karo Syrup
½ cup water
2 cups sugar
Boil as for icing
Two Eggs (whites, beaten stiff)

Pour syrup over whites gradually. Flavor.

Frosting
(Bowman Family)

1 cup sugar
1 tablespoon vinegar
3 tablespoon water
2 egg white

Cook sugar & vin. & water very slowly until it spins a thread. Have white of eggs beaten stiff. Pour this over egg whites & beat.

BUCKEYE FROSTING BOILED
(Bowman Family)
———•◦•———

Whites of three eggs beaten to a stiff froth, one large cup loaf sugar (or granulated). Moisten with four tablespoons hot water. Boil sugar bristly for five minutes or until it "jingles" on the bottom of the cup when dropped into cold water or ropes or threads when dropped from end of spoon. Then with left hand pour the boiling syrup upon the frothy eggs in a small stream, while beating hard with right hand. If preferred add half a lb sweet almonds blanched and pounded to a paste, or a cup of hickory nut meat chopped fine & it will be perfectly delicious. This amount will frost the top of two layer cakes.

MARSHMALLOW ICING
(Bowman Family)
———•◦•———

2 coffee cups granulated sugar
½ lb fresh Marshmallows
2 eggs
1 cup cold water
1 teaspoon vanilla

Dissolve sugar in water in sauce pan. Cook until it strings. Beat the whites. Add Marshmallows cut in small pieces, then pour over in the boiling candy. Beat hard until cool enough to spread on cake. Add vanilla. Reserve enough marshmallow to decorate cake. Cut them in half.

CREOLE COOKIES
(Bowman Family)

2 cups of sugar, 1 cup of sweet milk, whites of 3 eggs, ½ cup of butter, ½ teaspoon of extract, 2 ½ teaspoons of baking powder, flour to form a soft batter.

Cream sugar & butter. Add milk & flour in which has been sifted the powder. Beat hard then fold in the whites. Pour into baking pan & bake a light brown. Ice with plain or colored icing.

MOLASSES COOKIES
(Bowman Family)

⅔ cup boiling water
⅔ cup Butter
1 cup sugar
1 cup molasses
5 ½ cups of Flour
½ Teaspoon salt
1 Teaspoon soda
Ginger
Cinnamon

Pour water over shortening. Add sugar & molasses. Stir until sugar dissolved. Add sifted dry ingredients. Mix well. Roll ¼ inch thick. Bake on greased cookie sheet in hot oven 10 or 12 minutes.

PUDDINGS, PIES, ETC.

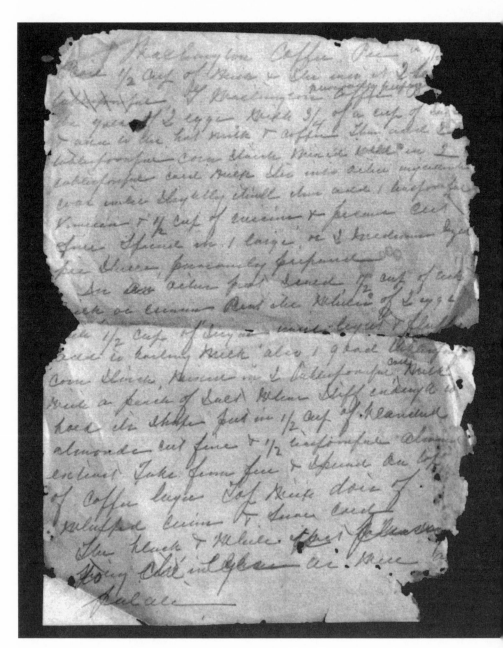

Receipt for Washington Coffee Pie (Bowman Family).

AUNT LIZZIE'S BLACKBERRY PUDDING
(Bowman Family)

Wash & pick over 1 quart of fresh berries, then put these in a saucepan with ¾ cup of sugar. Let the berries heat very slowly to boiling point, stirring now & then to prevent scorching, but do not mash the berries. Have ready a thin simple cake batter, made of 2 eggs beaten together, 1 cup of sugar, ½ cup of butter, 2 cups of milk, 2 cups of sifted flour, ½ teaspoon of salt, 2 teaspoons of baking powder.

Directions
Cream the butter & sugar add beaten eggs. Add the dry ingredients sifted together alternately with the milk. Add 1 teaspoon of vanilla, beat 3 minutes (This batter should be the consistency of waffle batter). More milk may be added if necessary. Pour the boiling hot berries into a baking dish, then pour the batter zigzag fashion through the berries. Put baking dish in a pan of hot water (about ⅓ up the side of baking dish) & bake in moderate oven until nicely brown. Serve with plain cream or make a hard sauce flavored with nutmeg.

LEMON DELICACY
(Bowman Family)

2 tablespoon butter
¾ cup of sugar
Juice 1 lemon, Grated rind
½ lemon
1 cup milk
2 tablespoons flour
2 eggs

Cream butter, add sugar & cream well together. Add well beaten egg yolks, flour, lemon juice & rind. Mix thoroughly. Add milk & fold in stiffly beaten egg white. Pour into greased baking dish. Set in pan of hot water & bake in a slow oven about 45 minutes. A delicate crust will form on top & the pudding will supply its own juice.

LEMON PUDDING
(Bowman Family)

Grate the rind of three lemons. Beat the yolks of 12 eggs and whites of 1. Put in 1 pt of cream, ½ lb of sugar, ½ lb of melted butter. Beat all together and boil.

BAKED PINEAPPLE PUDDING
(Bowman Family)

Drain the juice from canned crushed pineapple. Butter a pudding dish & place in the bottom of it a layer of split ladyfingers, moistened with pineapple liquor. Put in a layer of the crushed fruit sweetened to taste & cover with more ladyfingers, moistened with pineapple juice. Have the top layer of the dish of pineapple & sprinkle with crushed macaroons. Put in an outer pan of boiling water & bake ½ hour.

PINEAPPLE SUM
(Bowman Family)

Soak ½ a box of gelatine in a scant cupful of cold water for one hour. Peel a small pineapple & grate it, then cover with a cup of sugar and let it stand for one hour before stirring the soaked gelatine into it. Turn all into a saucepan, set within a pan of boiling water, and stir until the gelatine and sugar dissolve. Remove from the fire & let it cool but not stiffen. Whip a pint of cream very stiff. Stand the saucepan containing the gelatine & pineapple in a deep bowl of cracked ice and as the mixture stiffens, beat into it by the spoonful the whipped cream. Beat steadily until all the cream is in, and the jelly is stiff and white. Turn into a glass bowl and set in the ice for some hours. Serve with Cream.

COTTAGE PUDDING
(Bowman Family)

¼ cup of Butter
⅔ cup of sugar
1 Egg
1 cup milk
2 ¼ cups of Flour
4 teaspoons of Baking Powder
½ teaspoon of salt

Directions
Cream butter, add sugar gradually and egg well beaten. Mix and sift flour, baking powder, & salt. Add alternately with milk. Turn into Pudding pan and bake 35 minutes in moderate oven. Serve with sauce.

DATE PUDDING
(Bowman Family)

One pound dates, two cups breadcrumbs, four eggs, one quart sweet milk, 1½ cups of sugar, & one-half cup nuts. Remove seeds from dates & chop fine. Cream yolks of eggs with sugar until light. Add chopped dates & breadcrumbs, stir well, then add milk & nuts. Nuts may be omitted if desired. Bake in a moderate oven. Take out & cool. Spread meringue made by whipping the whites of the eggs stiff & adding four tablespoons of sugar on top & bake in a slow oven until light brown.

CASTILIAN PUDDING
(Bowman Family)

Soak ¼ of a box of gelatine in ¼ cup of water. Put into a small saucepan 4 tablespoonfuls of boiling water, 2 squares of unsweetened chocolate, & ¾ of a cup of sugar & stir till smooth, then add another ¾ of a cup of boiling water & boil all 5 minutes. Pour over the dissolved gelatine, stir well, strain & cool, then add 4 tablespoonfuls of sherry, a tablespoonful of vanilla, & as it begins to thicken, fold in the stiff whites of 3 eggs. Put into a mould and let it stand overnight. Serve with whipped cream.

QUEEN PUDDING
(Bowman Family)

1 qt of new milk
1 pt of bread crumbs
1 Cup granulated sugar
Yolks of 4 eggs
1 tablespoon butter
1 teaspoon extract of lemon

Mix well, pour into pudding dish, cook until done. Then spread with a layer of fruit jelly. Beat eggs to a froth with 1 teacup of sugar. Add a little lemon juice. Meringue the pudding & cook a brown color. serve with a rich sauce.

INDIAN PUDDING
by Miss Bella Bowman

Have ready on the fire a qt of milk boiling. Stir slowly into this two large tablespoons of fine cornmeal & boil a little while to thicken. Remove from fire. Add half a cup of sugar, the well-beaten yolks of two eggs, & flavor with vanilla or nutmeg or any preferred flavoring. Just as you put into stove add the well-beaten whites. One hour will be required for baking. Serve with hard sauce made by creaming well two tablespoons of butter & one light cup of sugar. If available, a little sherry makes a delicious addition.

CORN PUDDING
(Bowman Family)

1 doz large ears of Corn split down the middle of the grain and cut it off. Add 4 beaten eggs, pepper and salt to the taste, one qt of milk if the ears are very large, less if small.

MACCAROON PUDDING ICED
(Bowman Family)

Line a mould with macaroons, as described for Iced Cabinet Pudding. Fill mould with Dried cherries, seedless raisins, and macaroons in layers; then pour a little madeira or sherry wine over them, and finish by pouring over all a custard of a pint of milk, 2 eggs, and flavoring to suit. Sweeten with ½ lb white sugar and in summer cover mould up in ice and salt until wanted. In winter steam it and serve with butter and sugar sauce.

CHARLOTTE RUSSE
(Martha Turnbull)

Dissolve an ounce & a half of gelatin in warm water, add to it two tumblers of new milk. Boil this until reduced one-half. Beat the yolks of six eggs with ½ lb of powdered sugar, pour the boiling milk upon the eggs & sugar, stir it well, and return to saucepan. When it begins to thicken, stir in the whites of the eggs, well beaten. Take the mixture off the fire and set it aside to cool. Froth a quart of cream & add when perfectly cool. Season with extract of vanilla.

Charlotte Russe

(Bowman Family)

Boil 1 pt of milk with ⅓ box of gelatin. Beat the yolks of 4 eggs with ½ lb sugar. Pour the boiling milk over and stir until thick as custard. Let it get cold, stirring occasionally to prevent settling. Season a pint of rich cream, put on ice, and whip to a stiff froth. Mix with the custard and pour in moulds lined with cake. Lady fingers are best.

Dandy Pudding

(Bowman Family)

1 qt milk, 8 eggs, 1 tablespoon arrow root mixed with some of the milk. Mix the yolks with the arrow root. Sugar to taste. Beat until light. Pour the boiling milk on the eggs. Put in a well buttered dish. Whites of eggs, beaten light, spread on the top. Flavor to taste and bake 20 minutes.

Polly Penny Pudding

(Bowman Family)

A layer of grated bread
A layer of sugar
A layer of Cinnamon and nutmeg
A layer of Butter
A layer of thin sliced Apples

Repeat above til pans are full. Eat with sauce of butter and sugar.

OLD AUNTY'S BREAD PUDDING
(Bowman Family)

8 eggs beaten separately. Bread soaked in milk until perfectly soft & mushy. 2 teaspoonful of yeast powders. Thicken a bit with flour.

POTATOE PUDDING
(Bowman Family)

2 lbs mashed potatoes, ½ lb butter beaten until light, 1 lb sugar, 2 eggs, Rind and juice of a lemon. When the oven is ready, add the whites of eggs beaten to a froth,

POTATOE PUDDING
(Bowman Family)

6 eggs, 1 lb brown sugar, ½ lb butter, 1½ lb mashed potatoes, 2 nutmegs, 1 glass brandy.

SNOW PUDDING
(Bowman Family)

½ package gelatine dissolved in 1 pt of boiling water. Add juice of two lemons, glass of light wine, ⅔ lb of granulated sugar. When nearly cold add the whites of six eggs beaten to a stiff froth. Put in moulds. Eat with boiled custard.

BLANC MANGE
(Bowman Family)

To 1 qt rich milk or cream, ½ oz gelatin, ½ lb sugar, ½ lb almonds blanched and pounded fine with a little sugar to prevent oiling. Strain the boiling milk and gelatine over the almonds. Stir until nearly cold. Form in moulds.

CHOCOLATE BLANC MANGE
(Bowman Family)

To 1 qt calves foot jelly, ¼ lb grated chocolate and boiled in 1 pt of milk, sweeten and flavor to taste, add 1 pt of cream, and form in moulds.

CUSTARD PUDDING
(Bowman Family)

Yolks of 10 eggs well beaten and white of five. Boil 1 qt of milk sweetened and flavored with vanilla. Pour on the eggs. Grease the pan well and put ½ lb raisins, ½ lb Citron. Pour the custard in the dish and place small pieces of bread and butter on the top. Bake twenty minutes in a moderate oven.

Marangue Pudding we made
(Bowman Family)

1½ pint of bread crumbs, 3 pints of milk, 1 doz eggs (keep the white of 8 eggs for the top), 3 cups of sugar. About one quarter pound of butter. Beat sugar and butter together. Flavor the white with the juice of one lemon, and the pudding with the rind. Beat the whites of the eggs to a stiff froth and put on the pudding after it is cooked, then put it in and let it brown. Sprinkle the pudding with granulated sugar.

Rice Marangue
(Bowman Family)

Little over one qt milk boiled with ¼ of lb of rice until quite soft. Then add a lump of butter the size of an egg and let remain until cold. Beat the yolks of six eggs with six tablespoonfuls of sugar. Then add rind and juice of one lemon, then add the cold rice. After beating well together, put in the whites of eggs well beaten with three tablespoons of sugar.

Hunting Pudding
(Bowman Family)

½ lb raisins, ¼ lb currants, 4 spoonfulls flour, ½ lb suet, 3 eggs, 1 qt milk, sugar, nutmeg, and grated breadcrumbs. Do not let the batter be too thick or too thin. When mixed stir in a wine glass of Brandy. Tie in a bag and boil two hours.

MINCE MEAT
(Bowman Family)

2 lbs beef, 2 lbs suet, 2 lbs raisins, 2 lbs currants, 4 lbs apples, 2 lbs sugar, 1 pt Brandy, 1 pt wine, ¼ oz Cinnamon, Cloves, nutmeg, 1 lb Citron

MONKEY PUDDING
(Bowman Family)

3 cups flour, 1 cup molasses, 1 cup milk, 2 cups suet, 2 cups raisins, 1 spoonful ginger, 1 teaspoon soda. Boil 2½ hours.

PLUM PUDDING
(Bowman Family)

1 lb of stale bread sliced cover with new milk until it soaks. 1 lb suet, 1 lb apples chopped fine, 1 lb raisins seeded, 8 eggs. Put in as much milk as will make a good batter. Beat all together and boil 3 hours.

COCOA PUDDING
(Bowman Family)

⅜ lb grated cocoanut, ¼ lb butter, ¼ lb sugar, wine & rosewater, whites of 6 eggs, baked in a crust.

LEMON PUDDING
(Bowman Family)

Grate the rind of three lemons. Beat the yolks of 12 eggs and whites of one. Put in 1 pt of cream, ½ lb of sugar, ½ lb of melted butter. Beat all together and boil.

RICE PUDDING
(Bowman Family)

Thicken ¼ pint milk with rice boiled dry, about 1 pint to which add 6 eggs, ¼ lb butter, ¼ lb raisins, 1 nutmeg. Bake one hour. Eat with sauce as follows: 1 lb brown sugar, 6 oz butter, 1 pt wine boiled. Pour over the above.

BOILED CUSTARD
(Bowman Family)

6 eggs, ¾ lb sugar beaten together. Then boil one quart of milk. Just before taking it off, put the rind of one lemon, then pour into the eggs through a sieve. Put all on fire and let it boil until somewhat thick, then put in the essence.

SMAI'S BAKED CUSTARD
(Bowman Family)

3 eggs
1 pt of milk
Some nutmeg grated in ½ teaspoon of butter
3 tablespoonfuls of sugar

BAKED CUSTARD
(Bowman Family)

1 qt of milk
5 eggs beaten light
Whites & yolks separately
5 tablespoons sugar mixed with the yolks
Nutmeg & vanilla

Scald but not boil the milk. Add by degrees to the beaten yolks and when well mixed stir in the whites. Flavor & pour into a deep pan. Set this in a pan of hot water, grate nutmeg upon it, & bake until firm.

CARAMEL CUSTARD
(Bowman Family)

Heat 3 cups of milk in a double boiler. When this is heating, caramelize 1 cup of sugar by pouring into an iron kettle in a heap & stirring constantly over a hot fire until it is a golden brown. Then pour slowly into the hot milk, stirring constantly. Next add 4 beaten eggs, a pinch of salt, & a little nutmeg. Boil 5 minutes, cool, & set on ice to become cold.

PEACH FOAM
(Bowman Family)

Fold the stiffly beaten whites of 2 eggs into three heaping tablespoonfuls of peach pulp. Sweeten to taste. Mix in a few seedless raisins & serve with whipped cream. This is a physical culture recipe much in favor.

PEACH CREAM
(Bowman Family)

Mash & sift a dozen ripe peaches. Dissolve one tablespoon of powdered gelatine & two or three cupfuls of sugar in a cupful of boiling water. When partly cooled stir in the peach pulp & add one-half a cupful of whipped cream. Chill in a mould. This may also be served as a salad with mayonnaise dressing, only be sliced & molded in the gelatine.

MISS MOLLY THOMPSONS LEMON PIES
(Martha Turnbull)

2 Cups white sugar, 3 Lemons, 1 Cup butter, 5 Eggs. The Whites beat fine. 5 small tablespoonfuls of white sugar. Put on the top of the pie, return it to the oven, after the pie is baked.

LEMON PIE
(Bowman Family)

Put together 3 teacups white sugar and a piece of butter the size of an egg. Add the yolks of 8 eggs well beaten, then the whites. Rind of 3 lemons and the juice, which mix with ½ cup Brandy. This will make 2 pies.

PINEAPPLE PIE
(Bowman Family)

Pare, remove the eyes, & grate 1 large pineapple. First allow three-quarters of a pound of sugar, ¼ of a lb of butter, 5 eggs, ½ pint of cream. Beat the butter, sugar, & yolks together until light. Add gradually the cream, grated pineapple, & the whites of the eggs, beaten to a froth. Line two pie plates with puff paste, fill them with this mixture, & bake thirty minutes in a moderate oven. Serve with soft custard.

FOOLISH PIE
(Bowman Family)

Whites of 2 eggs, a can of peaches, 1 cup of whipped cream, and 2 tablespoon of sugar. Beat the whites stiff, then add sugar & beat 2 minutes. Layer spread in a pie pan and bake till brown. Let the merangue get cold, then spread the drained sliced peaches over it and top with whipped cream. Serve sliced like any other pie.

CHOCOLATE PIE-WITHOUT PASTRY
(Bowman Family)

Melt 1 large square of bitter chocolate, (1 oz) with 1 tablespoon milk. Add 2 Egg yolks and ¾ cup sugar and beat well. Then add 1 cup warm milk in which 2 tablespoon of butter have been melted. Pour into a small pie plate (nine-inch size) and bake in a slow oven until thick. Cover with merangue made from whites of egg and 2 tablespoons of sugar. return to oven and brown. Serve cold slice in a pie fashion.

If you will—

Remember to dip the cake knife in cold water each time before cutting cake; the slices will be smooth & regular and the icing intact.

Peach Cobbler
(Bowman Family)

Make a dough as follows: mix & sift 4 cups of flour, 1 teaspoonful of salt, & 4 teaspoonfuls of baking powder. Cut & rub in half-cup of butter & lard mixed. Then add one quarter of a cup of milk. Mix thoroughly & roll out to fit a deep baking pan. Pare and stone a quart of ripe peaches, place in the dough, then sprinkle over all two cups of sugar. Roll the dough which came from the trimmings, cover the top, & cut a few notches to allow the steam to escape. Then cover the top & bake for an hour. Serve with sugar & Cream.

Washington Coffee Pie
(Bowman Family)

Boil ½ cup of milk & stir into it 2 teaspoonfuls previously prepared G. Washington coffee. Beat the yolks of 2 eggs with ¾ cup of sugar & add to the hot milk & coffee. Then add 2 tablespoonfuls corn starch mixed well in 2 tablespoonfuls cold milk. Stir into other ingredients. Cook until slightly thick, then add 1 teaspoonful vanilla & ½ cup of raisins, & pecans cut fine. Spread in 1 large or 2 medium-sized pie shells, previously prepared.

In an active pot saved, ½ cup of rich milk, or cream. Beat the whites of 2 eggs with ½ cup of sugar until light & fluffy. Add to boiling milk also 1 good tablespoonful corn starch, mixed in 2 tablespoonfuls cold milk with a pinch of salt. When stiff enough to hold its shape, put in ½ cup of blanched almonds cut fine & ½ teaspoonful almond extract. Take from fire & spread on top of coffee layer. Top with dots of whipped cream & serve cold. The black & white is pleasing to the eyes as well as the palate.

CRANBERRY PIE

(Bowman Family)

Blend one can of sweetened condensed milk with ¼ cup of lemon juice. Add the yolks of 2 well-beaten eggs, 1 cup of strained Cranberry pulp. Pour into a baked pie crust. Cover with a meringue made from the whites of eggs. Bake in a moderate oven 10 minutes or until brown. Chill before serving.

FAMILY PIE PASTRY

(Bowman Family)

Mix and sift 2 cupfuls of flour, ½ teaspoon salt. Measure ⅔ of a cupful of lard, and take out 2 tablespoonfuls. Work the remainder with flour using the tips of fingers. Moisten with ½ cupful of cold water. When thoroughly blended, toss ⅔ of the dough on a slightly floured board. Pat and roll into rectangular shape. Spread with 1 tablespoon of the reserved lard and dredge with flour. Cut in halves lengthwise & pile strips on top of another. Fold in halves lengthwise then in quarters. Again pat & roll out as before. Spread with remaining lard, dredge with flour, & fold as before. Cut in halves & turn over as to have the cut edges come on top. Pat & roll each piece to fit in top of pie. Pat & roll the reserved dough into under crusts.

PIE CRUST (GOOD)

(Bowman Family)

2½ Cups of sifted flour
1 Cup butter & lard in equal proportions
1 heaping teaspoon of baking powder
A pinch of salt
½ Cup of ice water

Have dough stiff & mix as little as possible. This makes two pies.

ICE CREAMS & ICES

Maccaroon Pudding Iced.

Line a mould with macaroons as Described for Iced Cabinet Pudding. Fill mould with Dried cherries, seedless raisins & macaroons in layers; then pour a little Madeira or sherry wine over them, & finish by pouring over all a custard of a pint of milk, 2 eggs & flavoring to suit, sweeten with ¼ lb. white sugar & in Summer cover mold up in ice & salt until wanted, in winter steam it & serve with lemon & sugar sauce.

Receipt for Maccaroon Pudding Iced (Bowman Family).

GOOD ICE CREAM
(Bowman Family)

1 egg to each qt of milk
¾ teacup of sugar
1 dessert spoon of corn starch

PEACH SHERBERT
(Bowman Family)

Add a scant pound of sugar to a quart of very ripe peaches crushed & passed through a sieve or colander. Add to this the unbeaten whites of 5 eggs & freeze. This makes a dainty dessert.

STRAWBERRY ICE
(Bowman Family)

To a qt of strawberry juice or pulp add a pt of syrup & the juice of an orange or lemon. Mix all well together & freeze. When the ice is well frozen, work into it a meringue mass made of the well-beaten whites of two eggs & an oz of pulverized sugar. Stir this well into the ice then let it harden.

Pineapple Sherbert
(Bowman Family)

Boil together a qt of granulated sugar & a qt of water until a thick syrup is formed & pour this very hot over a can of grated pineapple. Add the juice of four lemons. Place the mixture in the freezer & add a pt of cold water. Just as the sherbert begins to freeze add the well-beaten whites of three eggs & finish freezing. Or two tablespoons of gelatin may be dissolved in enough of the water to cover, then add the mixture before freezing.

Pineapple Ice
(Bowman Family)

Select two ripe pineapples, and to them allow a qt of clarified sugar & a lemon. Pare & grate the pineapples & press the pulp, of which there should be not less than a qt, through a sieve. A small quantity of the pineapple should be reserved to be finely sliced & added to the ice when half frozen. Stir the pineapple pulp into the clarified sugar & lemon juice & freeze. When frozen add the whites of two eggs which have been previously beaten to a stiff froth & mixed with four tablespoonfuls of powdered sugar. Mix these thoroughly with the ice & set it aside to harden. The best ices are prepared by first cooking the sugar into the form of a syrup & then adding the fruit; when cool freeze.

CANDIES

Aunt Lizzie's Blackberry
Pudding

Wash & pick over 1 qt of
fresh berries — then put them
in a sauce pan with 3/4 cup of
sugar — Let the berries heat very
slowly to boiling point stirring
... & then to prevent scorching
but do not mash the berries
Have ready a thin simple
cake batter — made of 2 Egg
beaten together
1 cup of sugar — 1/2 cup butter
2 cups of milk, 2 cups of
sifted flour — 1/2 teaspoon
of salt —
2 teaspoons of baking
powder

Directions
Cream the butter & sugar
add beaten Eggs —
Add the dry ingredients

Receipt for Aunt Lizzie's Blackberry Pudding (Bowman Family).

COCOANUT CREAM BARS
(Bowman Family)

Pour ½ a cupful of rich milk over one cup and a ½ of sugar. Add 2 tablespoons of butter and boil just 12 minutes. Now turn in ½ a teaspoon of vanilla, ⅓ of a cupful of shredded cocoanut. Beat rapidly until creamy & pour out on a buttered pan. Cut into Bars when cold. These bars will be better the day after they are made as the longer they stand the more tender the cocoanut becomes & the more creamy the candy. Don't be afraid to send these by mail

COCOANUT FUDGE
(Bowman Family)

2 Cupfuls sugar
¾ cup of milk
1 Teaspoon vanilla extract
2 Tablespoon of Butter
1 Cupful shredded Cocoanut

Direction
Boil the sugar & milk well as in fudge receipt, adding the butter after the mixture has been cooking ten minutes. Stir in the cocoanut, also the vanilla, continue cooking for five or seven minutes longer. Remove from the fire and beat until creamy. Pour into greased dish & mark in squares when cold.

Egg Kisses Mrs H
(Bowman Family)

Put the unbeaten whites of 3 eggs in a bowl & add 1½ teacups granulated sugar & 1 teaspoon of vanilla. Beat until very stiff, then drop a spoonful at a time on greased paper placed on top of a stove pan. Set in a moderate oven to bake.

Pecan Slices
(Bowman Family)

½ lb whole Pecans
1 lb Brown sugar
4 eggs
1½ cups of flour
1½ teaspoon Baking Powder

Break eggs into a bowl. Add sugar and beat up together til thick. Add flour sifted with the Baking Powder and the whole pecans. Turn into a flat, buttered and floured cake pan and bake in a moderate oven for 25 minutes. Allow to become cold then cut into slices.

PECAN NOUGAT

(Bowman Family)

Stir together one and one quarter lbs of pulverized sugar, 1 lb of glucose, and one-eighth lb of gelatine dissolved in a little hot water. Whip or beat the mixture until it becomes light and white, then stir in slowly 1¼ lb of sugar, which has been boiled until it forms a ball when dropped from spoon in water. Now mix in thoroughly 1¼ lb of chopped pecan meat, not very fine. Line a box in the bottom and sides first with ordinary writing paper, then with paraffin paper & pour in the candy, pressing it down to form a smooth compact mass. Lay paraffin paper on the top and set aside to become cold and dry. The nougat may be slipped from the box and sliced with a sharp knife. The slices should be wrapped in paraffin paper.

DELICIOUS NOUGAT

(Bowman Family)

Melt over a slow fire 1 cupful of granulated sugar with a few drops of lemon juice. Let it boil slowly & when it "threads" when dropped from a spoon, beat in a ½ cupful of blanched & chopped almonds. Rub the pattie roller & board or table with olive oil; cut the candy very thin. Then with a knife also dipped in olive oil cut the candy into diamonds & when quite cold serve to your friends.

Stuffed Dates
(Bowman Family)

Fill with a mixture made as follows:

Put into an agate saucepan 1 cupful of granulated sugar & a gill of cold water with half a salt spoonful of Cream of Tartar. Stir just long enough to dissolve the sugar. Then boil without scorching until a drop put into cold water can be formed into a soft ball. Remove from the fire immediately. skim off every particle of [illegible] and pour the syrup into a bowl. When so cool and thick that the finger leaves a dent when pressed upon it, stir with a wooden spoon to a white paste; when too stiff to stir with a spoon knead the mixture with the hands. This filling will keep for weeks. When you wish to use it set the bowl containing it in a pan of hot water until cool enough to handle.

Divinity Candy
(Bowman Family)

In a saucepan put ⅔ of a cup of water, 3 cups granulated sugar, 1 cup of syrup. Allow to boil until the mixture makes a soft ball when tested in cold water. Twenty minutes after the first saucepan has been started, into a second saucepan put ½ cup of water, 1 cup of granulated sugar. When this mixture threads, it is done. This will be very nearly the same time the first is in proper condition. When the first is ready the mixture should be poured slowly over the whites of 3 eggs whipped to a stiff froth, beating briskly all the time. When it has reached a satisfactory stage, turn in slowly the contents of the second saucepan, still beating constantly, & stir in a cup of nuts. Turn the mass out in a buttered tin & cut in squares when cool.

PEANUT BUTTER FUDGE

(Bowman Family)

To make this fudge: Put two cups of sugar & two-thirds of a cup of sweet milk in a saucepan & boil until a soft ball is formed when tried in cold water, then remove from the fire. Add 4 tablespoonfuls of peanut butter, a few grains of salt, & 1 teaspoon of vanilla. Beat until creamy, add one-third of a cup of chopped raisins, turn into a buttered pan, & when cool, cut into squares.

CHOCOLATE CAROMELS

(Bowman Family)

¼ lb Bakers Chocolate grated, ¼ lb Butter, 1½ lb of Brown sugar, 1 teacup of cream, season with vanilla, cook 20 minutes.

WALNUT CHOCOLATE

(Bowman Family)

Melt in a cup of cream 4 cups of granulated sugar. Boil them on a hot stove for five minutes. Place the saucepan in a vessel of cold water. Pour into the mixture a teaspoon of vanilla, stir the mixture until it is firm enough to form into shapes. Make into spheres or balls and dip them into melted chocolate. Lay half a walnut neatly on the top or on the side.

Fudge (good)
(Mamie Fort Thompson)

2 cups sugar
2 tablespoon corn syrup
⅔ cup cream
⅔ cup chocolate
Vanilla
1 heaping tablespoon butter
pinch salt

Mix sugar, corn syrup, other until ingredients are blended. Cook to soft boil stage. Remove from fire & set in cold water. Add butter and allow to cool.

Miss Kleinpeter's Candy Receipt
(Bowman Family)

1 lb of 4x sugar to the white of one egg & 1 tablespoon of water, to thickness of biscuit dough, ½ tablespoon of extract. Work well & roll flat then form into shapes.

Author's Note: "4x" means powdered sugar. "X" is a symbol for fineness.

Home made Candy
(Bowman Family)

Take six cups of granulated sugar, 3 cups of water, ½ a cup of vinegar. Boil them until the mass is waxy. Remove from the fireplace in an earthenware bowl & stir until creamy. Do not stir while boiling. Have ready a lot of nuts of different kinds & fruit. Mix with the candy, which has been rolled on a greased marble board. Cut the nut filled candy into slices. Some may be colored with cochineal.

SYRUPS, PRESERVES, & JELLIES

Receipt for Coffee Jelly (Bowman Family).

A HOME MADE SYRUP
(Bowman Family)

Put 1 cup of granulated sugar in a frying pan or iron skillet and melt without any water, stirring constantly to prevent burning. When melted, have ready 1 pt of boiling water-& add it immediately. The sugar will at once form a hard cake, but the water will run under it & keep it from burning. Add a ½ cupful of sugar and boil until the hard sugar is all dissolved. The results will be a rich golden brown syrup.

PEACH SYRUP
(Bowman Family)

4 pts of water are poured over 4 lbs of Peaches & boiled until the fruit is tender, then it is formed into a sphere & pulp rubbed through to remove the pits. To each pt of the juice, add a lb of sugar & the whole brought to a boil. It is then sealed in hot bottles & put away for future use.

LEMON SYRUP
(Bowman Family)

12 lbs of crushed sugar
25 lemons

Add to the sugar enough water to make a thick syrup and boil until it is thick as molasses. Four qts is sufficient and don't forget the egg shells to clear it. Pour it into a vessel to cool. Grate the rind of 15 lemons, tie it in a muslin bag, and drop it in the syrup. Let it remain all night. Squeeze the juice from all the lemons and pour into the syrup; mix well. Bottle, cork, and seal.

OAKLEY WATERMELON RIND PRESERVES
(Bowman Family)

Pare the rinds, soak them about twelve hours in fresh water; change the water. A short time before cutting putting a small lump of alum. Line the bottom and sides of the kettle with fig leaves. After cutting the rinds into fancy shapes, place them in the preserving kettle, sprinkling alternate quantity of pulverized alum between each layer, then cover well with fig leaves. After with cold water, and let them simmer or boil slowly till tender. Take them from the kettle & drop them into cold water while preparing the syrup. For the syrup [use] almost two or three pounds more sugar than the weight of fruit or you will not have syrup enough. And to each pounds of sugar allow an ordinary coffee cup of water. Let it boil up twice, clearing with the shell & beaten white of an egg. Then put in the rinds and let them boil all clear. If the syrup is not thick, let it boil a little longer after taking out the preserves. For flavoring, simmer the peal of a lemon & some pieces of ginger root in the water with the rinds; transfer the ginger root to the syrup & squeeze in the juice of two or three lemons.

PLUM PRESERVES
(Martha Turnbull)

The plums should be nearly ripe. Weigh them and allow one pound of sugar for every pound of fruit. Put the plums in a stone jar. Boil the syrup until you have removed the scum, then pour it boiling hot over the plums. The next day pour it off, boil, & pour back over them. The third day boil fruit & syrup in the kettle until done. The scalding prevents the skins from coming off.

PEACH PRESERVES
(Bowman Family)

1¼ lbs of Peaches
1¼ lbs of Sugar
1½ pt of water

Boil sugar more than for Figs. Skim well, add peaches, and boil fast until done.

GREEN GRAPE JELLY
(Bowman Family)

This is to be served only with meats & is of a most delicate color. Do not gather the grapes too green, & if a few are slightly turned it will do no harm. Stem the grapes with the skins on, adding very little water as the fruit is rich in juice. Allow a 1½ lb of sugar to every pt of juice. The jelly is of a light green color.

QUINCE JELLY
(Bowman Family)

If a very light jelly is desired the seed should not be put in, but if they are omitted the juice must be boiled 30 minutes. Allow only ¾ of a lb of sugar to a pt of juice.

Mrs Leake's Cocoanut Jelly
(Bowman Family)

1 cup of cream
1 cup of sugar

Boil until thick; when cool add the cocoanut.

Fig Preserves 1919
(Bowman Family)

To a pint Jar:
1 ¼ lb of Figs after pealing
1 lb of sugar

Directions
Boil sugar with 1 pt or over of water. As soon as scum rises skim &
put in Figs, which have been hardened in Lime water four hours then
rinsed & washed in clear water. Boil fast and steady until clear &
done.

Coffee Jelly
(Bowman Family)

½ a box of gelatine soaked in about a cup of cold water for one hour.
Add a pt of strong hot coffee and 1 cup of sugar. When dissolved
strain into a mold & put on ice. Serve with whipped cream.

CREAM JELLY

(Bowman Family)

Let the calves feet stock become perfectly cold, then carefully remove every particle of grease. Melt the stock and to a qt of rich stock add a full qt of rich cream. If the weather is very cold more cream may be added. Stir the cream and stock together and continue to stir always in the same direction until nearly cold. Add a wine glass of Marischino or Trojan cordial. Sweeten to the taste. Dip the Moulds in cold water and pour in the jelly as soon as it begins to thicken, or then before. In flavoring care must be taken not to use too much of the extract, exercise your judgment about it.

PICKLES

Receipt for Green Pepper Pickles (Bowman Family).

Recipe to make Yellow Pickles
(Sarah Turnbull Bowman)

Take 1 lb of good ginger, 1 lb of garlic, 2oz long pepper, 1 pint black mustard, and 1 oz tumeric. Lay the ginger in clear water until it is soft enough to slice; change the water every day. Prepare the pepper in the same manner, lay in the garlic in strong brine 3 or 4 days. Skin them nicely, then rub them with salt and dry them in the sun 2 or 3 days. Then wash them in clean water and dry them in the sun. The tumeric and mustard seed are pounded. Put all these ingredients in a three gallon jar with 1½ gallons of good cider vinegar. Stir them well and set the jar in the sun-until the Pickles are ready. Shake it well every day and keep it closed. Lay your Pickles in a strong brine until they turn yellow which will probably be a week (be particular in washing them well when they are gathered). When they are yellow, dice and bleach them in salt and water in the jars. When they are bleached soak them in clear water 1 day and night. Then put them in a dye of tumeric and vinegar and let them stay until they are well dyed, then wipe them and put them in the prepared vinegar. The Cabbage is to be sliced scalled 3 days in succession. Change the water each time. The best way is to sprinkle salt over the cabbage and pour boiling water on it, then rub them with salt and dry them in the sun 2 or 3 days. Lay them a few hours in fresh water, then put them in a dye of tumeric and vinegar a week or two and put them in the prepared vinegar to be kept closely covered and and stand for several months. Add strong vinegar to it as you find it necessary. Mama puts 2 oz of cloves, 2 of allspice, and 1 of mace in the prepared vinegar. White wine vinegar is as good as cider.

Sweet Cucumber Pickles
(Bowman Family)

1 qt of small cucumbers, 3 cups of sugar, 3 cups of vinegar, ⅓ cup of green nasturtiums seed, six whole allspices, small piece of stick of cinnamon. Select cucumbers of uniform size about 3 inches long measure in qt jars. Wash well & put to soak overnight in brine made with a qt of water in which ⅓ of a cup of salt has been dissolved. Next morning rinse well & wipe. Put sugar, vinegar, & spices to boil. Then put in a cucumber. Heat thoroughly & place in sterilized jar in a dozen cucumbers then a sprinkle of nasturtium seed. This gives a flavor like dill. Continue heating the cucumbers & pack snugly in the jar. After the addition of each cucumber add a sprinkle of nasturtium seed until the jar is full. Boil the syrup & pour over the cucumbers boiling hot. Fill the jar full to the top with the hot syrup. Put on new rubbers & top and seal while hot.

Green Pepper Pickles
(Bowman Family)

The bell peppers are the best and should be gathered when quite young. Slit the side & carefully take out the core, so as not to injure the shell of the pepper. Then put them into boiling salt & water, changing the water every day for one week, & keeping them closely covered in a warm place near the fire. Stir them several times a day. They will first become yellow & then green. When they are a fine green put them into a jar, first stuffing them as for do mangoes & pour cold vinegar over them, adding a small piece of alum.

CHOPPED PICKLE
(Bowman Family)

1 Gal. Cabbage
1 Gal. Tomatoes green
1 Qt. Onions
two green pepper pods

Chop cabbage & tomatoes fine, can pass onions after slicing through a meat chopper, light sprinkling of salt over all, mix well & put in a sack to drain overnight. Put in a porceline kettle with three table-spoons full of white mustard seed, one of ground ginger, one of cloves, one of mace & cinnamon, 1½ of tumeric powder, 5 cts worth of Celery seed, two cups of sugar. Mix well & cover with good vine-gar. Simmer slowly until tender.

You can use more sugar if you like them sweet, sprinkle the salt the same as if you were going to serve them on the table.

I wish you success
H E T

FRENCH PICKLE
(Bowman Family)

½ peck of green Tomatoes, 6 large white onions, 1 large Cabbage, 6 green peppers, 2 tablespoonful allspice, 2 do cloves, 2 do salt 1 tea-spoonful of mace, ½ lb white mustard seed, 6 tablespoon brown sugar. Put the whole into a preserving kettle, cover with vinegar, and let boil three hours.

Oyster Pickle
(Bowman Family)

Take the oysters from the liquor, strain and boil it. Rinse the oysters if there are any bits of the shell attached to them. Put them into the liquor while boiling. Boil them one minute, then take them out of it and to the liquor put a few pepper corns, cloves, and a blade or two of mace, add a little salt, and the same quantity of vinegar as oyster juice. Let the whole boil fifteen minutes then turn it on to the oysters. If you wish to keep the oysters for a number of weeks, bottle and cork them tight as soon as cold.

To Pickle Tomatoes
(Bowman Family)

Take a peck of tomatoes, the small round ones are best for pickling, and prick every one with a fork. Put them into a broad stone or earthen vessel, and sprinkle salt between every layer of tomatoes. Cover them and let them remain three days in the salt. Then put them into vinegar and water mixed in equal quantities half and half and keep them in it twenty-four hours to drain out the saltiness. There must be sufficient of the liquor to cover the tomatoes well. To a peck of tomatoes allow a bottle of mustard, ½ of cloves, ½ of pepper. With a dozen onions sliced thin, pack the Tomatoes in a stone jar, placing the spices and onions alternately with the layers of tomatoes. Put them in til the jar is two-thirds full. Then fill it up with strong cold vinegar and stop it closely. The pickles will be fit to eat in a fortnight. If you do not like onions, substitute for them a larger quantity of spice.

PICKLED ONIONS
(Bowman Family)

Put small white pickling onions, which have been peeled in a jar, with about a teaspoonful of whole spice to each jar. Boil cider vinegar allowing 1 tablespoonful of brown sugar to each qt of vinegar. Let it cool and fill the jar until the onions are covered. Air tight jars are not necessary but the bottles must be corked well.

PICKLED PEACHES
(Bowman Family)

To a pk of cling peaches, 3 qt vinegar, 1 lb brown sugar, ½ pint Brandy, ½ oz cloves, cinnamon, mace, ginger. Mix all together pour hot over the peaches. Set in the sun 3 weeks.

MANGOES PICKLING
(Bowman Family)

Take oval shaped young melons. Cut a piece out of side & extract the seed. Then (having tied on the pieces) put them in strong salt & water for two days. Afterwards drain & wipe them, put them into a kettle with vine leaves under & over them, & a small piece of alum, & hang them on a close fire to green. Keeping them closely covered to retain the steam which will greatly accelerate the greening. When they are quite green, have ready the stuffing which must be a mixture of scraped horseradish, mustard seed, onions, cabbish celery seed, pepper, mace & nutmeg if liked. Fill the mangoes with this mixture putting a small clove of garlic into each. Replace the pieces at the opening, tie them tightly. Put them into stone jars, pour boiling vinegar over them, & cover them well.

Alum is very useful in extracting the salt taste from pickles & making them firm & crisp. A very small quantity is sufficient. Too much will spoil them. Vinegar & spices for pickles should be boiled but a few minutes. Too much boiling makes it lose strength.

MENUS

Menu for Mr. Jenning's Visit (Bowman Family).

SMAI'S LUNCH
(Bowman Family)

First course: Raw Oysters, white wine
Second course: Oyster Gumbo
Third course: Fried Oysters
Fourth course: Turkey & Tongue, French Peas, & Ground Artichokes
Fifth course: Salad
Sixth course: Gelatine, Cakes, Floating Custard, Candies, Champagne
Salted Almonds, salted pecans, olives, pickles served during the meal.

MRS LEWIS' LUNCH
(Bowman Family)

First course: Boiled cold shrimp
Second course: Deviled Crabs
Third course: Cauliflower on toast
Fourth course: Chicken salad
Fifth course: Roast Turkey & sliced tongue, Olives, & salted Almonds
Dessert: Ice Cream, nuts, & Cake

Mrs Lewis' Lunch
(Bowman Family)

First course: Turtle Soup, Pickles, Olives, Almonds
Second course: Baked Fish, potatoes mashed, Saratoga chips
Third course: Shrimp with mayonaise dressing decorated with sliced tomatoes, small water crackers
Fourth course: Roast Beef, Broiled chickens, Vegetables
Fifth course: Fruit, then Ice cream, & cakes, French Candies
Wines during dinner: Sherry goes with soup, White wine with fish, Claret after this & with the roasts, Champagne during the rest of the dinner, also dessert, but Sherry can be used with nuts.

(Bowman Family)

First course: Gumbo
Second course: Fish & Potatoes
Third course: Stuffed oysters & Crackers
Fourth course: Turkey, Rice, Peas, Artichokes
Fifth course: Asparagus
Sixth course: Dessert
Seventh course: Coffee

MENUS FOR MR. JENNING'S VISIT
(Bowman Family)

Breakfast

Friday, June 7/94
Broil chickens, Hominy, biscuit, Saratoga chips, Waffles, Maple Syrup

Saturday
Broil ham, Hominy, Muffins, Scrambled eggs, Batter cakes.

Sunday
Steak, Roles, Irish potatoe croquets, Waffles

Monday
Bacon, Omelet, hominy, Muffins, Batter cakes

Tuesday
Broil chickens, Saratoga chips, hominy bisquit, Waffles, Maple Syrup

Dinner

Thursday, June 6
Roast chickens, & Steak, Rice, Potatoes, Okra, macaroni, Squash, White cake, Blackberry pies, & Bavarian cream

Friday
Ducks & ham, Rice, Potatoes, Squash, beets, tomatoes, Sweet potatoes, White cake, pudding, & blackberries

Saturday
Broil chickens & ham, Rice, Potatoes, macaroni, peas, Snap beans, beets, Chocolate cake, & Bavarian cream

Sunday
Turkey, Steak, Rice, Sweet Potatoes, Squash, tomatoes, potatoes-carrots, Ice cream, & chocolate cake

Monday
Broil chickens, Rice potatoes, macaroni, Beets, Squash, Snap beans, Sweet wafers, plum pies

Tuesday
Roast chickens & fried, Rice, Sweet Potatoes, beets, macaroni, potatoes & carrots, Sponge cake cocoanut pies, & snow custard

The last of my list:

Supper

Thursday, June 7
Tongue, crackers, Roles, biscuit, cake, orange preserves, cird [curd]

Saturday
Ham, crackers, biscuit, Waffles, Strawberry Preserves, Sweet wafers

Sunday
Broil chickens, wafers, bisquit, cake, Strawberry preserves, cird

Monday
Broil chicken, wafers, bisquit, cake, Waffles, plum preserves, & cird

Mr Jenning's first visit remained from Thursday, June 7, until Tuesday, June 12, 1894.

Author's Note: The discrepancy in the dates was made by the Bowman family.

DINNER COURSES

(Bowman Family)

First course: Oyster Cocktail & Salted Crackers, a little sprig of celery on the side of the plate
Second course: Oyster Gumbo
Third course: Stuffed Crabs, Parched pecans, Stuffed Dates, Chicken Salad
Fourth course: Roast Turkey, Rice, French peas, Artichokes, Cranberry Sauce
Fifth course: Asparagus
Sixth course: White Fruit Cake, Kisses, Orange jelly decorated with whipped cream & Sliced Oranges, Coffee

PAPA'S BIRTHDAY DINNER, 1920

(Bowman Family)

First course: Oyster cocktail & salted crackers
Second course: Oyster Gumbo & Rice
Third course: Stuffed Crabs & Crackers
Fifth course: Chicken Salad, Parched pecans
Sixth course: Roast Turkey, Rice, Peas, Artichokes, Cranberry Sauce
Seventh course: Stewed Oysters, Crackers
Eighth course: Coconut cake, Plum pudding, Jelly

Author's Note: The missing fourth course was a mistake or omission made by the Bowman ladies.

Papas Birthday Dinner, 1923
The 91 anniversary
(Bowman Family)

First course: Oyster Cocktail & salted crackers
Second course: Oyster Gumbo & Rice
Third course: Red Snapper, Tartar Sauce, Irish Potatoes, Parched Pecans
Fourth course: Roast Turkey, Rice, Peas, Artichokes, Candied Potatoes, Cranberry Jelly, quince jelly, Pickle, Chicken Salad
Sixth course: Stewed Oysters & Crackers
Seventh course: White Cake with Candles, Fruit Pudding, Chocolate Cake, Cherry Jelly & Coffee

Author's Note: The missing fifth course was a mistake or omission made by the Bowman ladies.

Papas Birthday Dinner, 1926
(Bowman Family)

First course: Oyster Cocktail & Salted Crackers
Second course: Oyster Gumbo & Rice
Third course: Red Fish, Irish Potato
Fourth course: Roast Turkey, Rice Peas, Artichokes & Candied Potatoes, Salted Pecans, Cranberry Sauce, Quince Jelly
Fifth course: Fruit Pudding Birthday Cake, Chocolate Cake, Jello
Sixth course: Coffee

EGGS NEEDED
(Bowman Family)

10 Eggs for the White Cake
3 for the Layer Cake
3 for the Pudding
3 for the Icing of White Cake
2 for the Fish

---

21 Eggs needed for Papas Birthday dinner 1924.

For Further Reading

Blassingame, John W. *The Slave Community: Plantation Life in the Antebellum South.* New York and London: Oxford University Press, 1972.

Brady, Patricia. *George Washington's Beautiful Nelly, The Letters of Eleanor Custis Lewis to Elizabeth Bordley Gibson, 1794-1851.* Columbia: University of South Carolina Press, 1991.

Editors of *American Heritage Magazine. The American Heritage Cookbook and Illustrated History of American Eating & Drinking.* American Heritage Publishing Co., 1964.

Egerton, John. *Southern Food: At Home, on the Road, in History.* Chapel Hill: University of North Carolina Press, 1993.

Faust, Drew Gilpin. *Mothers of Invention: Women of the Slaveholding South in the American Civil War.* New York: Random House, 1997.

Floyd, William Barrow. *The Barrow Family of Old Louisiana.* Lexington: n.p., 1963.

Fox-Genovese, Elizabeth. *Within the Plantation Household-Black and White Women of the Old South.* Chapel Hill: The University of North Carolina Press, 1988.

Harris, Jessica B. *The Welcome Table: African-American Heritage Cooking.* New York: Fireside Books, 1996.

—. *Iron Pots and Wooden Spoons: Africa's Gifts to New World Cooking.* New York: Fireside Books, 1999.

Hearn, Lafcadio. *Lafcadio Hearn's Creole Cookbook.* Gretna, La.: Pelican Publishing Company, 1967.

Jones, Katherine, M. *The Plantation South.* Indianapolis: Bobbs-Merrill Company, Inc., 1957.

Kane, Harnett T. *Plantation Parade: The Grand Manner in Louisiana.* New York: William Morrow and Company, 1945.

Randolph, Mary, Plaskitt and Cugle. *The Virginia Housewife or, Methodical Cook.* New York: Dover Publications, Inc., 1993.

Saxon, Lyle. *Old Louisiana*. New Orleans: Robert L. Crager &
Company, 1950.

Schmit, Patricia Brady, ed. *Nellie Custis Lewis' Housekeeping Book*.
New Orleans: Historic New Orleans Collection, 1982.

Spratling, William, and Natalie Scott. *Old Plantation Houses in
Louisiana*. New York: William Helburn Inc., 1927.

Tucker, Susan. *Telling Memories Among Southern Women—Domestic
Workers and Their Employers in the Segregated South*. New York:
Schocken Books, 1988.

INDEX

214 FAMILY RECIPES

Cranberry Pie, 171
Cream Jelly, 191
Cream Sponge Cake, 130
Creamed Oysters in Toasted Cups, 95
Creole Cookies, 150
Croquettes, 99
Crumb Cakes, 132
Cup Cake, 132
Cup Cake (Mrs H), 132
Custard Pudding, 163

Dainty Toast, 113
Dandy Pudding, 161
Date Pudding, 158
Delicious Apple Fritters, 81
Delicious Dixie Biscuits, 68
Delicious Nougat, 181
Delicious Waffle Recipe, 124
Deviled Oysters, 94
Divinity Candy, 182
Dixie Spice Cake, 145
Doughnuts, 124
Doughnuts (Mrs H), 125
Dr Brooks, 65

Egg Kisses Mrs H, 180
Eggless Mayonnaise, 59
Eggs Baked in Tomatoes, 114
Eggs for Breakfast, 113

Family Pie Pastry, 171
Fannie Williams Rolls, 74
Fig Preserves 1919, 190
Fine Waffles, 123
Fish, 93-94
Fish Salad, 93
Fish Sauce, 93
Foolish Pie, 169
Fowl, 97
French Pickle, 197
Fritters, 79
Fritters Mrs Montague, 79

Frosting, 148
Fruit Cake, 136
Fruit Punch, 119
Fudge (good), 184

Ginger Biscuit, 71
Ginger Cake, 143
Ginger Cake (Mrs H), 143
Ginger Pound Cake, 144
Gingersnaps, 151
Good Cake for Scarce Seasons, 142
Good Ice Cream, 175
Green Grape Jelly, 189
Green Pepper Pickles, 196
Green Tomato Soy, 108

Haden Sauce, 109
Hickory Nut Cake, 137
Highland Punch, 119
Home Made Bread, 64
Home made Candy, 184
Home made Syrup, 187
Hunting Pudding, 164

Ice Creams and Ices, 173
Indian Pudding, 159
Irish Potato Soup, 48

Jam Cake, 140

Ladies Icing Recipe, 148
Left-Over Turkey Gumbo, 47
Lemon Delicacy, 156
Lemon Pie, 168
Lemon Pudding, 156, 166
Lemon Syrup, 187
Lightning Cake, 131
Lobster Croquettes, 95
Lucy's Spoon Bread, 73

Maccaroon Pudding Iced, 160
Mamie's Receipt Gingerbread Soft, 67